Paid to Play

✦

The Business of Game Design

Keith A. Meyers

iUniverse, Inc.
New York   Bloomington

Paid to Play

The Business of Game Design

iUniverse books may be ordered through booksellers or by contacting:

iUniverse
1663 Liberty Drive
Bloomington, IN 47403
www.iuniverse.com
1-800-Authors (1-800-288-4677)

ISBN: 978-1-4401-0416-9 (pbk)
ISBN: 978-1-4401-0417-6 (ebk)

Printed in the United States of America

Dedicated to:

To my Mom who gave me my love of games
To my Dad who taught me persistence
To my Brothers who showed me what it meant to play well
To Michael and Cheryl who opened the door for me to this wonderful world
To Joyce and Colleen who have made the journey so much fun
To my Children who sat through countless play tests with smiles on their faces
To my Wife who chose to love an aspiring game designer

Contents

Intro

I've been playing games for as long as I can remember.

One of my earliest gaming memories is my aunts, uncles and cousins—a normally reserved bunch—gathered around a table yelling at each other and laughing while playing *Pit* one evening. This experience instilled in me a love of games and their ability to bring people together from all walks of life, giving us permission to be ourselves, and socialize in a truly joyous manner.

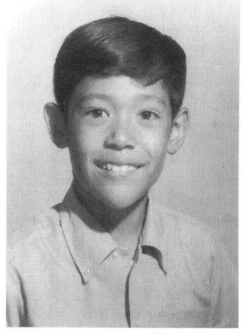

Keith Meyers, aspiring game designer

We had most of our large holiday gatherings at our house and it turned out that the best way to baby-sit all the kids was to get them playing games. As a result, every birthday and Christmas I received games that could be played with my numerous cousins.

I guess game inventing was in my blood. Whenever I got a game that I did not think played well enough, I adjusted the rules and added whatever was necessary to make that game a better game. Sometimes I would create an entirely different game from the parts I had available. I never imagined that there were people out there inventing games and making money. I assumed games came from some great creative depository in the sky.

The story of how I became a game designer began the same as many beginning inventors. It was the late 1980's and I was unsatisfied at work. I had this cool idea for a game but had no idea how to start. Not knowing how lucky I was about to be, I opened my phone book and looked up 'game companies'. Lo and behold, The Game Works was listed there. I gave the number a call and the President/Owner of the Company answered the phone (this was a SMALL company). I pitched my idea to him on the phone, and was politely told they did not make strategic games. We ended up chatting for a while though, and it turned out they needed someone to do some writing for them. It started out as a contract job, which later turned to a part-time job. Within 6 months, I was a full-time employee of The Game Works. Nirvana!

After several years, I had learned many things about the ins-and-outs of running a small game business which included game design, but also covered warehousing and shipping, accounting, overseas production, sales, etc., etc. As luck would have it, after several years, I moved next door, literally, to a position with a small chain of retail stores called The Game Keeper. They were opening their 12th store when I joined them. During the next decade, they grew into the biggest game-selling powerhouse in the nation, with up to 100 stores pushing out games by the baskets-full each Christmas.

I was in charge of store promotions, so anyone who wanted to promote their game went through me. I met a lot of key people at game companies. The Game Keeper had a big hand in making a lot of games successful and it opened my eyes to the fickle nature of the game consumer and how the success of a game did not necessarily depend on how well it played.

I worked at The Game Keeper for over a decade and the century was about to turn its counter over. The Game Keeper was purchased by Wizards of the Coast at the onset of the *Pokémon* trading card craze in the U.S. That was an outrageous time filled with armed guards, truckloads of trading cards, and long lines of salivating kids. Ultimately, Hasbro bought Wizards of the Coast. Within a few short years The Game Keeper retail stores would become a thing of the past. With some foresight, I crafted a small handful of game prototypes and used my many contacts to get them in front of game companies. I received three offers. That was what launched me on my full-time inventing path, and I haven't looked back. In 2002, realizing how fortunate I was to be doing what I was doing. I started teaching adult ed classes to help others get started with game inventing. Those teachings and my decades of hands-on experience are in your hands now in this first book, "Paid to Play: The Business of Game Design". I hope it helps you achieve much success!

Defining our Framework

WHAT IS A GAME?

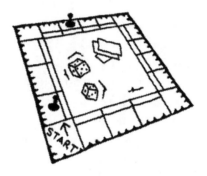

For me, a game is a means of getting people together for social connectivity. We most commonly see it in the form of board games, card games, and party games. Often they will be referred to as 'tabletop' games or 'traditional' games because traditionally games were played around a table. For the purposes of this book, they do not mean console or platform games such as PlayStation and Wii, nor do they mean computer games played on PCs and Macs, nor sports games played with sports equipment. I will use the term 'board game' generically to include card and party games unless I specify differently.

The dictionary defines a game as, "any activity undertaken or regarded as a contest involving luck, skill or a combination of both, and played according to a set of rules for the enjoyment of the players or

1

spectators." I think the key words to recognize here are 'contest,' 'rules,' and 'enjoyment.' A 'contest' implies there is a winner and that is true of all games. It might be one winner, it might be a team of winners, but in some manner there is a way of determining, through scoring usually, who wins. 'Rules' are also an essential element of a game. They create the playing environment from which players can strive to be that winner. Rules provide the structure and order necessary to determine that a player has actually won. And 'enjoyment'—probably the most obvious and overlooked aspect—means that players have to want to play… no fun, no game.

WHO PLAYS?

From my decades with the retail chain, The Game Keeper, it appears that roughly 25% of the population plays games. The game playing population is broad and varied.

Game players will range from ages 3 to 103. They will come from all educational backgrounds, with every cultural, ethnic, skill and personality mix imaginable. If we reduce it to the most general terms, however, there are more male game players, and the game playing age range is strongest in the 8–12 age range and also the 20- to 30-something age range.

For each segment in the gaming market, you will see game player traits specific to that market. For instance, the *bridge*-playing crowd tends to be 40+, while the *Dungeons & Dragons* role-players are late teens through the mid-20s. Strategic games are more male-centric while social party games lean more towards females. But these are just generalities and there are exceptions in every category. Suffice it to say, with the many hundreds of games released each year, there is a game for everyone.

WHY PLAY?

There are three main reasons for gaming: socialization, challenge, and hobby.

In socialized gaming people gather because they have something in common. It could be shared experiences (friends), shared relationships (family), or shared interests (groups, organizations, clubs, etc.)

It could be as simple as people wanting to interact with each other and gaming fits that need. It could be beyond simply interacting, they are hoping for an injection of something fun into their lives. Keep in mind that one person could find a challenging game of chess fun, while another expects fun to look more like a group of people acting silly while playing charades.

For a challenge in gaming, game players are usually looking for an experience that will stretch them in some manner. Often this could be in strategic thinking, but it also could take the form of expressions of creativity. The ultimate reward for a player looking for a challenge is that moment of triumph. That instance when they are recognized for their creative game play or their brilliance strategically. This moment can happen at any point during game play but it is most satisfying when it results in the player winning the game.

Many people play games because it is a hobby. With all types of hobbies, the activity serves as a way for people to bond with another over a common interest. On Yahoo Groups alone there are more than 25,000 groups in the U.S. devoted to board and card games. A game hobby can be unified over a specific theme such as war games, train games, word games, etc. or simply a group that meets regularly to play games.

To serve that market even more, adding some touch of collectibility, fuels the devotion of those hobbyists. It can be as blatant as *Magic: The Gathering*, the first collectible/tradable card game where cards are printed in varying degrees of rarity, and card packs offer an unknown variety of cards, making some cards more sought after and valuable. Or with the huge success of a euro-game such as *Settlers of Catan*, the variations and spin-offs keep coming and serve to feed the hunger of those fans and keep their gaming experiences fresh.

THE METAGAME PRINCIPLE

There are several definitions for the term "metagame" but for the purposes of this book, we will use the term to refer to the elements surrounding the core of game play.

An example familiar to everyone is American football. At the core of game play there are several players per team, a set of accepted rules, a football and a playing area. That's all that is needed to start up a game of street ball. When you step into high school or college ball, you add sports gear, coaches, referees, and nice fields. At the core, it is the same game, but somehow all these extras seem integral to playing school ball. And what about cheerleaders, and spectators? The game would still be football without them, but they certainly enhance the game and fit our expectations of what a game of football is. Now advance to professional football. We introduce the elements of stadiums, cities that host the team, sports commentators that call the play-by-play, the cameramen who capture the game and the media teams that broadcast it to the world. Again, football could and would be played without them, but they serve an essential  function for the modern-day version of the sport we enjoy today.

How does this all relate to a board game? All these extra bells and whistles comprise the metagame. These enhancements further our enjoyment of the game and motivate us to 'buy in' to the game and particular teams. We root for a team simply because we went to school there, are living there, or have some other affiliation with the team. We probably do not know anyone personally on the team and we may not be able to quote the stats for any given player but for some reason, we love the team. So how do you imbue that feeling into a game?

The best modern-day examples of games that demonstrate the metagame principle are *Cranium* and *Magic: The Gathering*.

Cranium features a bunch of mini-games in one bigger game. It contains word puzzles; drawing, sculpting, and acting activities; charades and musically-oriented performances; and it ranges in topics from music to history to math. It has something for everyone. Its brilliance is that at any moment during the game, there is a chance for someone to shine.

I am particularly good with word puzzles so that is where I would excel. My son is an actor so he leaps at the chance to do anything that involves standing up in front of others. My artistic daughter loves to do the sculpting and drawing activities. We all became invested in the game and our team because we all had moments where we could be great.

With *Magic: The Gathering*, the game consists of 5 types of magic each with its own slant. For instance, black magic is evil, red magic is destructive, and white magic is holy. From the thousands of cards available, you craft your own deck of 40 cards with which to play. With the unlimited (too large to count) combinations, you can customize your deck to reflect who you are. If you are a 'bash everything' player, or a 'super sneaky' player, or a 'defend and outlast' player, then you can build the deck of your dreams. The regular release of new cards promises to keep you busy refining your dream deck into eternity.

For inventors, it is important to consider creating a structure whereby players can make the game their own. This can take the form of giving player characters different personalities, offering many tactical strategies to win, having a variety of winning scenarios, and creating several playing frameworks such as multiple tracks or maps. Your creativity is the only limit, and your rewards might be selling tons of games!

Defining the Game Inventor

INVENTOR OR DESIGNER?

I am often asked whether I prefer to be called a game inventor or a game designer. I think of myself as a designer. Having seen and played so many games over my lifetime it is hard to believe I am 'inventing' something totally new. A new game for the most part is just bits and pieces of all the games that came before it, jumbled together, recombined, and repackaged. If you think of a painter, they are not inventing a painting. The brushes, paints, canvases, and images already exist. They are just using these tools to create their own vision. So like a painter, a game designer is using all the tools available to build a unique game concept.

TRAITS OF A GAME DESIGNER

If we look at the occupations of the designers of some of the world's bestselling games, we see no obvious common thread. *Scrabble* was created by an architect; *Candy Land*, by a schoolteacher; *Clue* was designed by a patent clerk; *Uno* by a barber; *Trivial Pursuit* was constructed by a pair of journalists; and *Pictionary*, by a waiter. I would bet they all had one common trait: curiosity. At one point in time they all asked themselves a common question that began, "What if...?"

I describe a game designer as a curious observer. Are you curious about the workings of various gizmos and gadgets? Have you ever broken down a process into steps and puzzle out why they are done in a specific order? Do you find yourself tumbling words around in your head looking for different/better/funnier ways to say things? Do you chuckle to yourself over strange combinations or juxtapositions of everyday items? If so, you are a curious observer... and you are only one step away from being a game designer.

The only real difference between a curious observer and a game designer is that the designer has taken something that interested them, something they thought was clever, unusual, funny, puzzling or unique, and created something new from it. It could be a physical prototype or simply a schematic in their mind but either way they have taken that fascinating element and put some structure to it.

Many of you reading might only be at the curious observer stage right now. By the time your reach the end of this book, you will have the necessary tools to get some of your curious observations out and into a concrete format and move into the formal designation of 'designer'.

SKILLS OF A GAME DESIGNER

A game designer plays a number of roles, and those roles require certain skills that will be useful if you want to pursue game design in earnest. None of the skills are absolutely essential but they make the task of building and selling games easier. This list is intended to make you aware of the skills that you already possess and where you might want to grow or seek outside support.

Game player – you need to play as many games as you can. As with the analogy of the painter earlier, the more tools and techniques you have in your bag of tricks, the easier it will be to achieve your vision.

Motivator – no one is going to make you create a game. This has to come from somewhere inside you; that curious observer that wants to hold something tangible in his or her hands.

Graphic designer – you are going to have to make cards, game boards and other game bits and you want them to be visually pleasing and laid out in a functional, simple and understandable way.

Writer – you will have to be able to write clear and concise rules, minimally. You may also need to create sales material, packaging copy, and news releases depending on whether you plan to license your game or self-produce.

Engineer – can you build a four-fold game board? If you dream up a *Mousetrap*-type game, can you prototype it? Be prepared to do so. Do not be afraid to seek help with more complicated designs. It will be well worth it if your end product performs flawlessly. Note: making a four-fold game board is covered in the chapter on prototyping.

Salesman – you are going to have to sell your game idea to game companies if you want to license it, or sell it to retail stores and the public if you self-produce.

Negotiator – getting the best licensing deal for yourself or getting the right manufacturing price for your game requires apt negotiating skills. As good as it feels to get your game to market, it feels a lot better when you make decent money as well.

Public Relations Person – be prepared to toot your own horn. Many people are too embarrassed or too humble to talk about themselves. Promoting yourself is an essential part being a successful game designer.

There are many more roles to tackle should you decide to self-produce your game. These additional roles are covered later in the book.

TOOLS OF THE GAME DESIGNER

To initially design a game, you can get by with items you have around the house, such as colored pens and pencils, a ruler, regular bond paper and cardstock, scissors, glue and tape, and game bits from other games such as player tokens, dice, a sand timer, and a spinner.

However, it is good to remember the better your first impression with your game prototype, the better it will be received. I recommend using a computer with a color printer for your card and board game graphics. As for computer software, you can get by with some proficiency with MSWord. You will need to know how to use tables and insert graphics. For your prototypes, illustration board found at most hobby and art supply stores is great for making game boards and cardboard tokens. Foamcore can be used for most other prototyping that requires more involved engineering. I would also recommend you invest in an X-acto knife and blades, a self-healing cutting mat, and a metal ruler that has a rubber or cork bottom. Some designers like to have a paper cutter on hand as well. Upgrade your adhesives to a paper glue; one that will not bleed through your paper printed with graphics. Glue sticks and double-stick tape may be useful as well. A digital camera will be extremely important in producing your final documents.

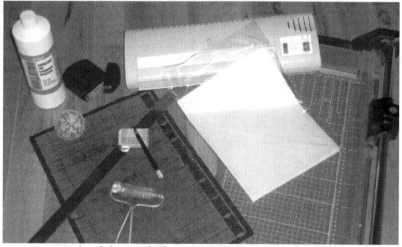

my tools of the trade for cutting, laminating and gluing

I am equipped to prototype just about anything. In addition to the items above, I have a large screen monitor, software that includes Photoshop (image manipulation), Illustrator and Freehand (vector-based drawing), a corner rounder found at most hobby stores, Rollataq glue and a hand applicator (note: described further when discussing prototyping), a heat laminator with laminating sheets, a video camera and the simple movie editing software called iMovie, a rotary cutter which is fantastic for cutting quantities of cards, and an ever-growing supply of game parts.

I find it extremely useful to peruse the aisles of Hobby Lobby and Michaels for pieces that can be used for games. Educational supply stores are also a great source, as well as, office supply and hardware stores.

LICENSING VS. SELF-PUBLISHING

One of the first big questions you will have to ask yourself is, "Do I want to license my game or publish it myself?" Here are some of the pros and cons to help you answer that question.

Licensing – basically, you are giving your permission to a game company to manufacture your game idea in exchange for a royalty. The structure of this 'permission', i.e. the contract, takes many forms and those aspects will be covered in more detail in the last chapter, "Success."

Pros: your job is focused on creating and selling your ideas. Once the contract is signed, you sit back and wait quarterly or twice yearly for royalty checks to come in. There is minimal cash outlay and this work can be done around other work schedules. You work at a pace that suits you and you answer only to yourself.

Cons: the manufacturer of the game gets final say in the look, feel and play of the game. If you cannot divest yourself of your creation and move on, this can be difficult to handle. Also, you have no direct effect on the sales of the game, so if it does not perform well, can you accept that?

Self-Publishing – this is all about running a business and having complete control of your own destiny. It is a massive undertaking, and you need to be up to the task.

Pros: your success is solely attributed to your efforts. You have complete control over every aspect of creating, producing, and how you sell your game. If you have success, you earn a bigger piece of the pie than if you licensed your game to another manufacturer.

Cons: after the initial creation of the game, running a business becomes the focus, so you will not revisit that initial creative period for some time. You, or someone you hire, must be good at package design and sales. Those are two factors that too often beginning publishers gloss over. I will state it again. *You, or someone you hire, must be good at package design and sales.* For as good as a game plays, and with all the enthusiasm you as the designer and manufacturer can direct at it, most games fail because they do not get into enough retail outlets (sales) or once there, do not sell (packaging). As a manufacturer, you need to be able to financially keep the company going minimally for three years while your game tries to get a foothold, without knowing whether you have a success on your hands. It has been said that the best way to make a small fortune in the game business is to start with a large fortune!

Both licensing and self-publishing are covered more fully in later chapters.

Do You Have the Right Stuff?

As for the decision to license or self-publish, it is often your personality type that is the determining factor. If you are still on the fence as to which way to go, take the following into consideration.

Those who license tend to be more introverted as they enjoy working at the computer or cutting cards or pasting up boards. Self-publishers need to be more extroverted in order to deal effectively with the store accounts, production offices, and shippers on a daily basis.

Licensors love the creative aspect of what they do and that is the most fulfilling part of game design for them. Self-publishers love the thrill of running a business and measuring their success by the sales that are generated.

Licensors are always ready to move onto the next creative project. Self-publishers need to continue to dot the i's and cross the t's on the one project, and then be ready to juggle when more products are introduced into the mix.

Both are their own bosses but the licensor generally has a much looser schedule and there is far less pressure to perform. For self-publishers, every aspect of the business has its time frames and there is daily pressure to keep the ship afloat.

Both models can make good money but if a game is truly successful, the publisher stands to make more because they take the larger risk.

Ask yourself, "What is my appetite for risk?" Should you play it safer by licensing your game, or take the risk of producing your own game?

Hopefully, the path for you is clearer now.

Now let's get started getting your game to market!

The Game Industry

TAKING AIM AT TARGET MARKETS

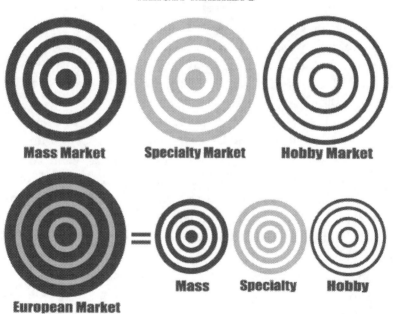

Few outside of the industry realize there are actually three very distinct U.S. gaming markets that cater to different types of gamers. As a designer, you can pick a market and design with that market in mind or you can design your game and then determine which market fits. The three markets are: the mass market, the specialty market and the hobby market.

It is important to know the difference because it determines the type of company to whom you pitch your game idea or, in the case of self-publishing, it determines your account base and your selling strategy. Your game will likely be suited for one of these markets and it is often a waste of energies to try to make, for example, a hobby market game fit into the mass market world.

Mass Market – this is the most familiar market as it is comprised of the five majors: WalMart, Target, Kmart, KB Toys, and Toys 'R' Us. While a huge quantity of games are sold through this market, only a very small percentage of games manufactured each year get to the masses.

Pros: if you are lucky enough to land a game here you could sell hundreds of thousands of games. And hundreds of thousands of games translates to a lot of money despite the cons.

Cons: this is a volatile market and cannot be counted on year to year. Your game could be a one-year splash or it could have a run of several years. However, it is unwise to get too comfortable with your sales in this market. Over the past decade 3 of the 5 (Kmart, KB Toys, and Toys 'R' Us) have had serious financial issues that only adds to the unpredictability of this market.

This is also the market where you, as a newbie to the toy and game industry, will have the least amount of clout. As an unknown inventor, getting your idea in front of a mass market game company such as Hasbro and Mattel would generally require using a broker or agent. If you are producing the game yourself, getting in the door is no small trick for a start-up company and, once in, their shipping demands and buy-back policies could prove to be too much of a financial obstacle.

Games launched in this market usually have a unique, visual gimmick that lends itself to a TV commercial. This means, in 10 seconds or less, you need to show the action of the game, have the consumer understand it, and be intrigued enough by it to seek it out on the shelves. Due to the large production run required for the mass market, these games can be budgeted and priced to accommodate the cost of plastic molded parts and electronics. This huge investment necessary to get these games on the shelves means there are only a handful of game companies that can service these markets consistently.

That being said, there are a number of games that find their way into the mass market after building up a substantial following first in the specialty market.

<u>Specialty Market</u> – this includes all the independently owned toy stores and game stores that cater to the every-day gamer. It also includes certain store chains, such as bookstores, sporting good stores, and drug stores, that sell games as a tangent to their core business. Although chains such as Barnes & Noble may be able to sell tens of thousands of games, most initial game production runs in this market are five to ten thousand.

Pros: this is the best way to grow a game into a successful best-seller. It is the path that *Pictionary, Outburst, Sequence, Apples to Apples* and numerous other board games have followed. There are many more companies servicing this market than the mass market, so there are more opportunities to license a game. Since sales levels are not as dramatic as in the mass market, it is a bit easier to gauge where sales are headed year to year.

Cons: it is a much smaller market so for the licensor/designer and the designer/manufacturer, getting a foothold can provide challenges. You are dealing with smaller ordering budgets and limited shelf space for which your game has to compete. Once you do get a foothold, it will generally be a 3-year build before you see just how good a seller your game is. The majority of the accounts you will be selling to will buy a dozen or half dozen games to start, so that means a lot of 'mom and pop' stores have to choose to carry your game for you to sell through an initial run of 5,000 games.

The games in this market are usually simple kids' games and adult games focusing on the social aspect of gaming. Most components are paper-based, with very little plastic.

<u>Hobby Market</u> – this market was spawned from the comic book stores back in the 1970's that started carrying role-playing games such as *Dungeons & Dragons* when they were first introduced. They later expanded to Collectible Card Games (CCG's) or Trading Card Games (TCG's) such as *Magic: The Gathering, Pokémon,* and *Yu-Gi-Oh.* This combined with collectible figures such as *Warhammer* lead the way

for the modern day hobby market store. Within the last two decades, these stores began increasing their offerings by carrying a selection of hobby games, usually called 'euro-games'. Euro-games come mostly from German-speaking countries where the gaming culture is very strong and games tend to be more strategic and decision-based. These same games may also be referred to as 'designer games' because there are several well-known game designers whose game creations are sought after much in the same way books by certain authors gain a following. The majority of these designers are from Europe where gaming is considered an honorable pastime.

Pros: there are a lot of companies to choose from so with persistence and a very good game design, you chances of licensing a game are high. And the fan base for hobby market games consists of very serious gamers, so word-of-mouth for a good game can spread quickly.

Cons: there is so much competition, with the shear quantity of games released each year that it is more challenging to get a foothold in the hobby market. Initial print runs of a game generally range from 1000 to 2500 units, so unless your game hits the right chord with game players, it is unlikely you will generate a large income stream.

The games in this market are more sophisticated than most U.S.-made games. The components are usually paper-based and will often include some nifty small wood components, such as cubes, people figures, etc. The production quality of these games is usually far superior to most American-made/Asian-made products.

<u>European Market</u> – this is more than another market, it is a territory made up of multiple markets similar to the U.S. Because the German-speaking countries have such a strong gaming culture, there are just as many game companies in Europe as there are in the United States. In 1843, when the first U.S. board game, *Mansion of Happiness*, was released, there were already 40 registered game companies in Germany. So, if you are looking for companies to pitch your idea to, opening yourself up to the European market can essentially double your opportunities. Despite the vast difference in population, it is just about as easy to sell 5,000 games in Europe as it is in the United States.

And like the different markets, individual European countries have different affinities for certain types of games. For example, the German-speaking countries prefer more thoughtful, strategic games with a focus on game mechanics, even in their kids' games. In France you can get by with lighter, sillier, social games, especially if they involve language. In Sweden you would be hard-pressed to sell a card game because that culture does not see the value in games using only cards. Beyond these generalities, the point is to remember that a game designed in the U.S. has potential to find a nice home in a European game company's catalog as well.

THE CUSTOMER'S PERSPECTIVE

I find it easiest to describe the game industry from the consumer's perspective, since it is a perspective we all share. So let us start there – on the black dot that says 'Game Player Consumer'.

We buy a game from somewhere; maybe it is a toy store or online or at a bookstore. As we move to the right in the diagram above, we see these and more options. The industry refers to this as a retail account. For each retail account there is someone designated as the Retail Buyer. If it is a large enough company, they may have several Buyers, but only one who is designated for buying games. This person evaluates all games to determine which ones are right for their store(s).

So how does this Buyer find the games to evaluate? As we move further right in the diagram, we see that Buyers get games from a variety of sources. They might see them at trade shows or in ads and other marketing channels or be called on by sales representatives or distributors. All of these efforts are coordinated by the game manufacturer/publisher.

And how does the game manufacturer come up with the games that they manufacture? If you are looking to self-publish your own game, you would be the inventor <u>and</u> the game company. At the more-established game companies, often a small percentage is designed in-house, usually by an R&D or Product Development team. The bigger percent come from outside sources… like you, the game designer.

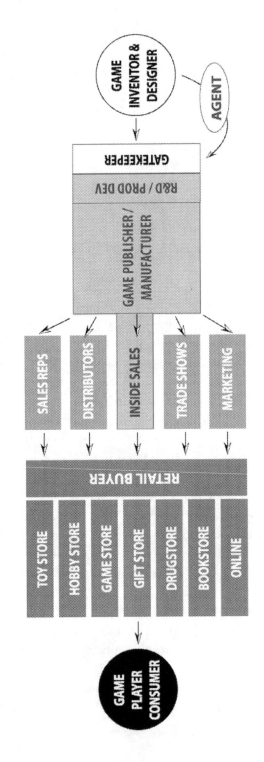

GAME INDUSTRY OVERVIEW:
HOW A GAME MAKES IT INTO SOMEONE'S HALL CLOSET

GAME INVENTOR & DESIGNER

AGENT

GATEKEEPER

R&D / PROD DEV

GAME PUBLISHER / MANUFACTURER

SALES REPS

DISTRIBUTORS

INSIDE SALES

TRADE SHOWS

MARKETING

RETAIL BUYER

TOY STORE

HOBBY STORE

GAME STORE

GIFT STORE

DRUGSTORE

BOOKSTORE

ONLINE

GAME PLAYER CONSUMER

And just like the retail accounts where someone is designated as the Buyer, there will be someone at the game company designated as the 'Gatekeeper'. There official title might be something different but their job, or one of their jobs, will be to make the initial judgment on whether or not a game idea should be brought in-house for further evaluation. For the biggest companies there is someone in charge of inventor relations and that is whom you are looking to reach. Unless you have established yourself in the industry in some way, you will likely need a broker or agent to get your game ideas in front of these large companies. Otherwise for most smaller companies, you can present your game ideas yourself, if you so choose. For medium- and small-sized companies, this 'Gatekeeper' could be part of the R&D team, or in product development, or a production coordinator or a multitude of other titles. Sometimes, and especially in the smallest companies, this person could be the President or Vice President.

For the majority of companies, the person looking at game submissions also has other roles they are performing at the company. Keep this in mind when you submit. You will need patience because your submission is usually not their highest priority at the moment.

THE GAME DESIGNER'S PIECE OF THE PUZZLE

The best news of all is that the toy and game industry really needs inventors and designers. We are the lifeblood of this happy, playful world. Without our brilliant, new ideas breathing creative life into the products that hit the shelves each year, the industry could not operate.

My conservative estimate is that 75% of all the games released each year come from the worldwide inventor community. As listed on www.boardgamegeek.com, there were more than 1,500 games released in 2007, not including game expansions. That means more than a thousand games each year need to be created by an independent designer. Why not you?

Where to Start?

THE 10 STEPS TO GETTING YOUR GAME PUBLISHED

There are 10 general steps that you will go through to get your game to market. The first six steps are related to developing the game and are the same licensing and self-publishing. The final four steps differ for licensors and self-publishers. The steps are covered briefly here with more details in this and subsequent chapters.

1. Conceptualize:

Develop your idea to determine where you are going with it. What is the game's name? What is the tag line? How do you envision the game playing? What is the market, the number of players and the age

21

range? Based on your concept, what physical game elements do you need to test it?

2. Build:

Initially, build a 'soft' prototype. Use scraps of papers with pen markings to emulate the cards, board and other game components. Does it look feasible? Next, create a 'hard' prototype which has components built to playable size and with a layout that is more formalized. Look for design issues and any game play problems. Aim for a final prototype with a full-color board, laminated cards, and full-scale components.

3. Play Test:

You can never play test too much. Initial play tests will determine if it even works and can be performed by you taking the roles of all players. Formal play tests use different groups to help you discover where your game needs improvement. Lastly, especially for hobby market games, try to 'break the game' by having players assume radical roles and strategies to encounter those potential one-in-a-thousand problems and issues.

4. Revise:

Based on your feedback and observations from play testing, determine which adjustments are needed to reduce flaws, create a better balance, and enhance or simplify game play. This is the perfect opportunity to use Game-storming techniques explained in the chapter on "Play Testing and Revisions".

5. Repeat steps 2–4:

This step may be repeated as many times as necessary to get game play to the best it can be.

6. Rules & Spec Sheet:

Write rules as the next-to-last step, before going to the very last stages of play testing. Use an impartial play test group to see if there is anything missing or unclear in the rules. The spec sheet outlines all the elements of the game on one page—it is useful for licensing your game or making sure you are on target and have all the elements completed when you head to production.

For Licensors

7. Inquire:

Start contacting game companies for whom you think your game will fit. You can inquire to multiple companies as long as you are willing to make prototypes for them all.

8. Submit:

Send your spec sheet followed by prototype and rules upon request. The prototype can be a game demo in CD-Rom or DVD format in certain cases. Whenever possible, arrange to pitch in person, as your enthusiasm for your own game cannot be matched by sheets of paper and cardboard bits.

9. Wait:

Patience is not only a virtue, it is a necessity. Depending on the time of year and company, this can be anywhere from a couple of weeks to months and months. For most people, this is the hardest step.

10. Sign:

It only takes one company to say 'yes' and make your game a hit. However, beginning and seasoned inventors alike will generally get rejections that outnumber the acceptances. Once you get the 'nod', negotiate a solid contract and listen for the sound. Can you hear it? Ka-ching!

For Self-Publishing

7. Source:

Call around to get best price for making the game. A one-stop shop is better than a dozen sources that have to be coordinated. Overseas (China) will be your best price but quality control and production and shipping time can be an issue. Finalize the graphics for all elements and make them print-ready.

8. Prepare:

Book and attend trade shows. Generate pre-sales and interest. Make sure bookkeeping, shipping, and warehousing are ready to roll. Get sales reps, distributors and all other resource and support personnel in the queue so when the game hits you can start running.

9. Produce:

Produce at the optimum time in the selling year cycle to decrease cash flow and promote sales success. Cross your fingers.

10. Sell:

You will likely get a lot of passes from buyers, but as long as you have games in your garage/warehouse continue to push your goods out the door. Word of mouth is the best salesperson, so get it on shelves in front of customers, whatever it takes. And then listen for the sound. Can you hear it? Ka-ching!

THE 3 CORE CONCEPTS

How did you get your first game idea? Chances are it started from one of three main concepts;

1. A Name or Phrase:

I was talking with some friends one day when one of them used the term, "Sitting Ducks." The phrase instantly conjured an exciting image of a shooting gallery with ducks in a row, scrambling to get out of the way. This was a great starting point. It was an active name, that ended up being called *Sitting Ducks Gallery* when published by Playroom Entertainment.

The phrase 'sitting ducks' helped bring many of the design elements together. Based on the name, I felt it needed an irreverent, tongue-in-cheek humor and it also made sense to develop the game as a line manipulation mechanic. The entire game came together in a matter of 3 days and sold to the first company to whom I presented it. Other games I have created starting from names and phrases include, *Spit It Out, Pecking Order* (re-named and re-themed *Tiki Topple*), and *Over and Out*. This is my favorite way to begin game design. Often, if I start creating a game using one of the other two following concepts, I will brainstorm the name immediately to see if it lends itself to other ideas in game play and design.

2. A Theme or Story Line:

I was driving in the car around the 4th of July when the deejay on the radio asked the question, "Who was the 2nd President of the U.S.?"

I was pretty sure I knew but as soon as I got home I looked it up to confirm—John Adams. I was intrigued by the fact that such an important historic figure was not a household name, simply because he was second. I started looking up other facts about 2nd's in our society: 2nd fastest animal, 2nd biggest state, 2nd man on the moon, etc. When I had gathered enough data, I crafted a game that became *2nd Guess*. That 'themed' game, and *The Hobbit: The Defeat of the Evil Dragon Smaug*, a 'story line' game, were the two that started me on my path of designing games full time.

3. Game Play/Thought Process

I was putting together a soundtrack for a Halloween party and I had a CD of animal sounds in the CD player. The first track was a cow mooing. When I heard the sound, I immediately knew what it was, but I wondered if it brought to mind the word 'cow' or the image of a cow. To test the concept, I created cards that had pictures on one side and matching words on the other. I used a tape recorder of scrambled sounds, and voilà, the basic game of *Ruckus* was born. The game launched first in Europe (and was renamed *Slammer*), is my second best-selling game to date and is still selling in numerous countries and languages.

Hue Knew? was another 'thought process' game based on the Stroop Effect, a scientific principle that proves that the brain processes colors at a different speed than it processes words. *Fast Figure* originated from a concept of game play where players are rushing to put general knowledge questions that have a numerical answer, in sequence.

THE CUSTOMER'S PERSPECTIVE

Here is an exercise I do in my game design classes. Close your eyes and picture a mystery game I am holding in my hands. I say nothing else and wait for the class to ask questions. What do you think the most common question asked is?

It is, "What's the name?"

Name recognition is one of the biggest factors in the consumer's decision to buy a game—or any commodity for that matter. A known game's name conjures up images from TV or our own personal experience while an unknown game's name offers us the first impression of what the game is about.

As we walk down the game aisle, the colors of the packages beckoning to us from every angle, it is ultimately the name that makes us stop and pick up the box. It has nothing to do with how well the game plays or how pretty the components are, it is simply whether the name strikes a chord. No matter how your game is created, take time to come up with the best name possible. The game's name could affect a game company's decision to give your game a serious look, and it could ultimately affect whether your game gets picked up off the shelf.

I also recommend putting time into coming up with a good tag line. The tag line, coupled with the game's name, should be strong enough to convince a consumer to turn the package over and read the back of the box. When *Apples to Apples* first appeared on the shelves in retail stores, the name and tag line read, "Apples to Apples, the frantic game of hilarious comparisons." That grouping of words told the would-be buyer that the game is funny, quick, and had to do with comparisons. I am sure that apt choice of wording went a long way to helping the game sell its millions.

THINKING OUTSIDE THE BOX, LITERALLY

Continuing with that train of thought, consider all the elements that you find on the outside of the box, besides the name and tag line. Be mindful of the number of players your game accommodates, their age range, how long it takes to play the game, and the category in which your game fits. You need to be aware of these factors for a couple of important reasons.

First, it is important to 'set the stage' when you pitch your game, either in person or by spec sheet (which is discussed in a later chapter). Your pitch should follow the process of examining a box as a game buyer would in a store. For example, start your pitch by saying, "This game is called *Grease Monkeys*, the dastardly and competitive game of race engine building [the front of the box], for 2–6 players, ages 12 and up. This is a strategy board game that takes about 45 minutes to play [side of the box]. The setting is the world of Formula One motor racing and....[back of the box]"

The second reason to be aware of these box elements is you are determining the scope of your buying audience. If you designed your game for left-handed Lithuanian female horseshoe makers named Greta, even if you sold your game to every single one of them, your sales will be minimal. Whereas, if your game works for 2–12 players, ages 6–106, can be played in half an hour, and is a broad, appealing topic, then you are giving yourself a good chance to sell lots of games. By being aware of these elements, you can start setting your expectations realistically.

side panel details from a Ravensburger game

GAME MECHANICS

The term 'game mechanics' refers to the detailed aspects of how a game plays. It is an accurate depiction because you will often find yourself tinkering with the game 'engine' to get it working just right. Occasionally you will have to perform a complete overhaul of the system to get things running again in the right direction.

Game mechanics are as numerous and varied as the designers who create them. To help you grasp the variety and multitude of options, I have compiled a list adapted from the boardgamegeek website with one or two examples of games that fit those mechanics. This list should serve to inspire and inform your game play decisions.

MECHANICS	GAMES		MECHANICS	GAMES
Acting/Performance	Charades, Cranium		Ordering	Racko, 10 Days
Action Point Allowance	Supremacy, Tikal, Torres		Paper-and-Pencil	Crossword
Area Control	Go, Blokus, Risk		Partnerships/Teams	Bridge, Charades
Asset Management	Settlers of Catan		Pattern Building	Tangrams, Score 4
Auction/Bidding	Modern Art, Bridge, Bohnanza		Pick-up and Deliver	Space Dealer, Rail games
Balancing	Jenga		Point to Point Movement	Sorry, Checkers
Betting/Wagering	Poker, Wizard card game		Puzzle Solving	Sudoku
Bluffing	Poker, Balderdash		Rock-Paper-Scissors	Ro-Sham-Bo
Campaign/Battle Driven	Diplomacy, D&D		Role Playing	Dungeons & Dragons
Chit-Pull System	Scrabble, Ra		Roll and Move	Parcheesi
Commodity Speculation	Monopoly, Acquire		Secret Unit Deployment	Diplomacy
Co-operative Play	Lord of Rings, Break the Safe		Set Collection	Canasta, Pit
Crayon Rail System	Empire Builder, EuroRails		Simulation	war, race, civilization, etc
Creative Writing	Balderdash		Simult. Action Selection	Apples2Apples, Hippos
Deduction	Clue, Coda, Mastermind		Singing	Name that Tune
Development	Civilization		Speed/Racing	Formula De, Winners Circle
Dice Rolling	Yahtzee		Storytelling	Ungame, Lifestories
Drafting	Magic: The Gathering		Tile Placement	Dominoes, Carcassonne
Drawing	Pictionary		Trading/Negotiation	Diplomacy
Hand Management	Hearts, Uno		Trick-taking	Bridge, Hearts
Hex-and-Counter	ASL, many war games		Variable Phase Order	Puerto Rico, Caylus
Memory	Memory, Husker-du		Variable Player Powers	Citadels, Cosmic Encounter
Modular/Changing Assets	Carcassonne		Visual Recognition	Set, Blink
Navigation	race games		Voting	Apples, Balderdash

My best recommendation for any game you are making is do some research to see what else is out there that has similarities to your idea. Play those games and make informed decisions about how your game might play and, hopefully, play *differently* from all the other games.

STRIKING A BALANCE

In almost every way, a game is about striking a balance. For instance making a game that is very complicated to learn but only takes 10 minutes to play is not a good balance. The effort is not worth the payoff. Likewise, creating a game that has a simple roll and move mechanic and lasts for 2 hours is also a poor balance in the opposite direction.

The areas of balance that you want to strike will be detailed in full in the section "What Makes A Good Game Good." In the early stages of game design, be aware that a game is not about one person, it is about all the players. Are you providing a satisfying and fulfilling game experience for all?

As a designer and a curious observer, be watching not only the choices people make and problems encountered during play tests, but watch the play testers themselves. If too many unrelated side conversations are taking place or players are getting up often to refill their drinks or powder their noses, these are signs that your game might not be holding their interest. Maybe there is too much time between players' turns or the game is lacking interactivity or possibly a combination of the two.

At each stage of game development, watch for the subtle signals that tell you that something could be better. Then ask yourself the question, "What if…?"

THE ROLE OF RANDOMIZERS

We are all familiar with spinners, dice and cards. Rarely do we give more than a cursory nod to how brilliant a role these randomizers play in our enjoyment of a game. To strike the right balance in a game, be aware of the role of randomizers and how they work, and how you can make them work for you.

Dice – As a teenager I was introduced to the role-playing game, *Dungeons & Dragons (D&D)*. It was an amazingly innovative concept—a story-telling game where the storyteller, the dungeon master, creates a scenario in which all the other players are inhabitants. Much of the game took place in your imagination, as the game components in the earliest days were merely paper, pencil and a bunch of odd-shaped dice. Everyone is familiar with the traditional 6-sided dice used everywhere, from the craps tables in Vegas to the board game on your dining room table.

My first copy of *D&D* included, in addition to the 6-sided die, a 4-sided, 8-sided, 10-sided, 12-sided, and 20-sided die. By creatively using these multi-sided dice, the game designers broke down everything that could occur in 'life' in the game scenario into percentages. If you wanted to fight someone, you referred to charts that took into account the weapons being used, the strength of the two characters fighting, the armor both were wearing, and their fighting experience. You then used the appropriate sided die and rolled it. It was a random roll, but with an outcome that took into account the specific scenario at that time.

In many young children's games, the roll of the 6-sided die is purely random and the subsequent result just as random, and for a 3-year old that is fine. As we 'evolve' as game players, we want our actions to dictate the outcome more and more. We want to see a balance in what should happen based on their choices; an action deciding an outcome, a choice with consequences, a roll and an appropriate result.

A 4-sided die allows for a 25% chance that a specific number will come up while a 20-sided die allows for a 5% chance. This means if your game includes one or more dice, you might be able to adjust the balance simply by switching to a different sided die… or by customizing one of the dice to strike the balance you need. Consider a 6-sided die; each side has a 1-in-6 chance of coming up on a given roll. If you put the number 1 on one side, the number 2 on two sides, and the number 3 on three sides, you now have a 50/50 chance of rolling a 3, a 2/3 chance of rolling a 2, and a 1-in-6 chance of rolling a 1. Imagine the possibilities with a 10-, 12-, or 20-sided die, the mathematical permutations are HUGE.

By using two different colored 10-sided die, you can generate a number anywhere from 1 to 100. Roll the two die—let's say a red and a white die in that order—and a resulting roll of 3-red and 7-white. That would be 37. A roll of 8-red and 2-white would be 82. Add a third die and you range from 1 to 1000. If you were testing a scenario whereby rolling a 35 or less would create a desired outcome, but the number combination was not coming up enough, you could adjust the target numbers instantly.

By using dice creatively, you can fine tune game play until you strike the right balance.

Spinners – Spinners also offer a complete array of percentage options. By dividing up the circle into any number of pie slices in various sizes of your choosing, you can create whatever proportions makes the best sense for your game. For example, it can be as structured as 4 equal-sized segments or as random as 11 segments; one that was 39 percent, another at 28 percent, two segments of 13 percent, three segments of 2 percent, and four at 1/4 of a percent.

Note that spinners are generally considered a children's game item. Past the age of 10, you should consider using other types of randomizers.

Cards – The main difference between using cards vs. dice and spinners is that one roll of a die or use of spinner once has no effect on the next roll/spin of the die/spinner. That is, if you roll a 3, you may roll a 3 on your next turn as well. Whereas when you draw from a deck of cards, the deck is reduced by one, and the card you drew is no longer available. Keep in mind that a die or spinner can lead to an unlimited, identical series of rolls or spins and cards result in a finite number of draws of a specific card.

The amazing thing about cards is that they allow you to use multiple attributes easily. Take a regular deck of cards, for instance. With four suits, 25% of the cards have a suit attribute. Two suits are red and two are black, so 50% of the cards have a color attribute. Each card in a suit has a different value, Ace through King, so 1/13 of the cards have a specific numeric attribute. Additionally, you can separate attributes by values of 10 (10, J, Q, K) or face cards (J, Q, K). There are the suicide king (hearts) and one-eyed jacks (club and hearts) thrown in for good measure. So you can see how a deck of your own design can have multiple attributes in whichever quantities or percentages you desire. Adjusting the balance can be as easy as adding or removing specific cards.

With all these permutations of percentages, attributes, and outcomes, it is easy to see why so many great game designers have a strong math background. One of the most prolific and well-known game inventors, Reiner Knizia, has a PhD in Mathematics. It is easy to see the beautiful mathematical balance he creates when playing his games. Another world-known game designer is Richard Garfield who holds a doctorate in Combinatorial Mathematics. His creation of *Magic: The Gathering* became a billion dollar industry within one decade and one only need play the game once to sense the mathematical balance on which the game designed.

Whether you are a math wiz or not, most issues of game balance, once you identify the problem, will be intuitive. Keep your eyes and mind open, and strive to find the perfect balance in all your games.

Prototyping

The Basic Rule of Prototyping

A common question from beginning game inventors is, "How good does my prototype have to be?" The basic rule of thumb is: create a prototype as good as you can with your available SKILLS, MONEY and TIME.

"The Hobbit" game   Prototype for "The Hobbit"

The soft prototype for your initial testing should be as simple and inexpensive as possible. Drawings on paper and cardstock should suffice.

Hard prototypes can range in price from zero dollars to hundreds of dollars; from pen drawings on pieces of paper and game bits you have around the house, to investing in a laminating machine, rotary cutter, glue rollers, and high quality color printouts. The parts that make up a prototype are generally fairly inexpensive as the costs for paper goods (the bulk of your game design) are readily available. The more significant expense is in the equipment to produce those paper components (see 'Skills and Tools'). If you intend on prototyping only one game, buying this equipment might not make a lot of sense; better to work with what you have. If you are looking at game design as a possible career path, or even an ongoing hobby, then all the gizmos and gadgets that are the tools of the trade will make your life easier and more fun.

Time can be a factor as well, especially as it pertains to your engineering and artistic skills and other available resources. If you do not have a color printer and a basic drawing program, chances are you will have to rely on someone else to produce the graphics for your boards, cards, and tokens. If you are not particularly 'handy' building a 4-fold board and a box to put it in could be quite an undertaking. Given your abilities and limitations, set a time limit for completing your prototype and do your best to stick to it. In an inventor's world, there are few hard and fast deadlines. Most are self-imposed time frames based on trade shows, meetings, and other industry events.

The main thing to achieve is building a game prototype with a look and feel of a playable game. The more the prototype enhances game play, the better. For *The Hobbit,* pictured above, there were strict constraints based on production time frames tied to a movie release, so many images were left out, the board was pieces of paper taped together and cards were not laminated. The quick mock-up, however, did not affect the game's playability which is what ultimately sold the concept.

WHAT DO GAME COMPANIES EXPECT?

Every game company will tell you they are buying the product (game play) not the package (quality of the prototype). The story of *Apples to Apples*, originally prototyped as *Apples to Oranges*, will illustrate this point.

| Apples to Oranges Prototype | with Apples to Apples box |

The original prototype was in a box that measured 22"w x 11"h x 4"d (too big for any store's shelf). It included a 2-fold game board, a set of plexiglass card holders, a mesh bag for holding a bunch of players pieces which were a collection of plastic animals, a box of 'oranges' cards and a box of 'apples' cards. Out of the Box Publishing, the company that eventually published the game, noticed in play testing that players had the most fun when they landed on the 'all play' space. Their stroke of brilliance was eliminating everything else and making the game about the two boxes of cards in a perpetual 'all play' mode. You can see in the picture above, the actual published box is the same size as the two smaller Apples and Oranges boxes combined.

Companies certainly do want content over appearance but if you are looking to successfully license your game consider these factors.

First Impressions – as with many things in the world, there is a judgment made based on appearances. When the exact same game is presented as a bunch of pencil drawings and as a computer-rendered group of graphics, you would naturally be predisposed to like the nicer rendering. You would already be on your way to liking it and hoping game play lived up to its look, whereas the pencil drawings might be a detractor from game play.

Representation – often the only direct communication you will have with companies will be by phone or email: so the prototype is a physical representation of you. Do you prefer being represented by a pencil drawing or a nicely executed piece of graphic art? Coming off as a professional goes a long way to getting your game reviewed and considered seriously.

Playability – games are supposed to be fun to play. A prototype that is sloppy and amateurish decreases the fun appeal of your game and presents an extra burden that your game play must overcome.

When a game company says they will look at any prototype, they are telling the truth. However, the better prototype you build, the better the concept and play of your game will come through, increasing your chances of success.

MAKING CARDS, BOARDS, BOXES AND BITS

When talking about components, no two games are alike. Describing how to find or create every type of component would be impossible, but here are a few design tips on the most commonly used components.

Cards – a standard poker-size playing card measures 2–1/2" by 3–1/2". You can decrease or increase either or both dimensions up to 1/4" and still maintain a good ratio for a hand of cards. If the cards are not going to be held in your hand, the size can be decreased to whatever dimension works for game play. Keep in mind that if young children are playing, cards that are tiny can be difficult for small hands to manage. Oversized cards can serve their purpose, but having to handle too many large cards can also be troublesome.

For standard poker-size cards, the following template works well.

CARD TEMPLATE

The back of the card is laid out upside down over the front of the card with four cards end-to-end all within an 8–1/2" x 11" sheet of regular bond paper. Print and fold across the middle horizontal line, lay down some glue between the halves, then cut along the card borders to create four playing cards. If you do not need card backs, you can lay out 2 rows of four cards and print on 110 lb cardstock. There is no folding, and this yields eight cards per sheet.

If you are creating cards to be held in your hand, putting a symbol or running a short word along the upper right and bottom left of the card (where the black '?' is shown in the image above) helps when the cards are fanned out. You cannot rely on the important information being only in the center of the card, as it is a challenge to hold all the cards so you can see the centers. If you can fit it in the design, it also helps to add the symbol/word where the grey '?'s are to make it easier for those who fan their cards in the opposite direction.

I recommend Rollataq brand glue available at most art supply stores. This glue applies thinly with no bleed-through. Rollataq also sells a hand applicator that is extremely easy to use when gluing lots of paper. I find the glue and applicator invaluable in my day-to-day work.

Regular bond paper when folded in half, glued and enclosed in a standard 3 mil laminate has a very similar weight and feel to standard playing cards. You end up with a similar end product when using 110 lb card stock, laminated but not folded. I am partial to heat laminate which uses laminate film with a slight, dry adhesive on the inside which is activated by the heat. You can use cold-press laminate sheets which have a peel away sheet revealing the tacky adhesive and does not need a machine, but the few times I have used the cold-press, the cards have come out slightly thicker. Not a big issue and, definitely for your first few prototypes, the cold-press would be more than acceptable. Some of my colleagues like the Xyron 'cold' laminating machines.

Boards – Modern day games do not come in the Monopoly-size box that housed a 2-fold board. The largest game boards are now 4-fold or 6-fold to fit in smaller packages. By current standards, you do not want a folded board to measure more than 10" square. This means when opened up, it would be a 20" square board. The method I use to create this size board is outlined as follows.

First, cut four 10" x 10" pieces of illustration board or foam core and place them together to form a 2x2 grid (step 1). Then take tape (I prefer Artists' Tape) and run a strip across the center division to secure all four pieces together and allow for a fold (step 2). Then run a piece of tape from the center of the board to the outer edge running perpendicular to the long piece of tape you first placed (step 3). Flip the board over or fold the board to make it easier to do this. And lastly, take your board

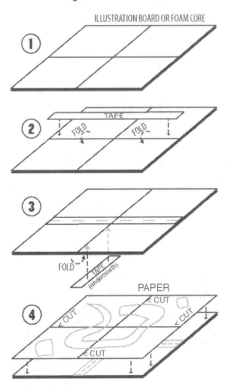

Making a Quad-Fold Board

graphic and cut it into 4 segments and glue each to the matching quadrant to the top of the illustration board (step 4). Test the board along the creases to make sure the graphic does not bind when folded. In building the board this way, when folded, all your graphics are on the inside where they will encounter the least wear and tear. For smaller boards just divide each width and length measurement by 2 to determine the size for each quadrant piece.

Boxes – I rarely build a box for my submissions as it is generally not important to game play. It will be changed by the manufacturer anyway when published. However, certain games such as *Niagara* and *Cleopatra and the Society of Architects*, both euro-games, make use of the box as a design element. If you decide you want a box or your game needs a box, here is the following step-by-step process for building a game box.

Determine the measurements for the box: width, length, and depth. For instance, to accommodate a 10" x 10" folded board, you might want a box that is 10.5"w x 10.5"l x 2.5"d. Pencil the layout onto a piece of illustration board, adjusted for your measurements (step 1). Make cuts along all the solid lines and only score (cut halfway through) the dashed lines of the illustration board. The scoring on the dashed lines allows for the board to fold, creating edges and corners.

Repeat the process to create the box top, but increase your width and length measurements by 1/4", and add finger cut outs (step 2) to help with removing the top from the bottom when together. Fold up sides (step 3) and use tape (I prefer artist's tape) to connect where the sides fold together. Glue printouts to box top and bottom that can then fit together as illustrated (step 4).

Making A Box

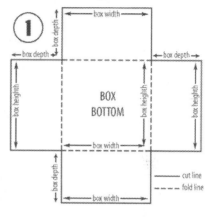

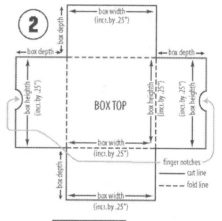

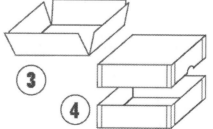

FAKING IT

So what do you do if you come up with a game idea that is beyond your scope to produce as a prototype? For example, if your game idea needs complicated engineering or electronic components, how to you portray that vision?

There are four ways to fake what you cannot do.

First, make detailed drawings of your 3-D vision. Creating a storyboard with clear images can describe your game nicely. This works best for in-person presentations but can be used as part of a Powerpoint presentation with narration if submitting via email or disk.

Second, you can emulate the hard-to-prototype element in another way. For one game, I had imagined a random sound generator; a device where pushing a button would start a random chain of mechanical noises or animal sounds to play at varying intervals. I used a tape recorder to emulate that sound generator. The sounds were not really random because I had programmed them onto the tape, but for one or two plays, it created that illusion. I later recorded the tape onto a CD-Rom. That made it a snap to duplicate for sending off to multiple game companies.

Third, make a video of what you have imagined. After all, movies are really nothing but simulated stories full of sound effects and graphic effects. Imagine that you are creating a low-budget film where your game idea is the star.

For one of my prototypes, I imagined an object that, when moved over a certain spot, would trigger a light to come on and a sound to be made. I filmed the piece being moved to the spot. Then a flashlight was turned on illuminating the spot from below, and a sound was made off camera. The shot perfectly illustrated the effect, as if all the electronics were in place.

If you make a video, script it ahead of time, and edit your piece if necessary. You can lose your reviewing audience quickly with long takes where you turn on the camera, walk in front of it to demo your game, wrestle with mistakes and do-overs, and then come back to turn the camera off. If you write a script in advance, you can match up shots with narration without a lot of extra footage that does not advance your presentation.

Fourth, borrow something from somewhere else. This can work really well for cards, boards, and boxes, as well as special gaming pieces. Call it repurposing. For cards, simply put adhesive labels over a regular card deck. For boards, find one the right size and glue your images to it. And for a box; recover a box that is has the right dimensions. With dice, you can glue little squares bit of paper on the sides to create new faces for the die. Poker chips can be used with graphics glued onto them for special tokens and pawns and other game pieces from any game can be re-used to serve the purpose you need.

Prototypes are all about facilitating game play without getting in the way. Parts and pieces you create or repurpose are completely allowable in the world of game design and prototyping.

Play Testing & Revisions

You can never play test too much or with enough different people. A big complaint I hear from game companies is that they receive games that have serious flaws in game play and unclear rules. Both are symptoms of inadequate play testing. As challenging as it can be at times, play testing is the best way to get valuable feedback needed to make your game the best it can be. Keep in mind that just because you imagine it is a great game, that does not mean it will play like a great game. Play testing repeatedly will prove your concept.

I am often asked how to get play test groups together. I find most game players are more than eager to play test a prototype. They feel like they are getting an insider's glimpse of the game industry. If you do not have or know of a network of avid gamers, you can usually find them through any number of group listings, such as Yahoo Groups, Google Groups, Meetup.com, etc. Posting flyers on a college campus offering snacks and beverages in exchange for play testers, and their valuable feedback, is an easy solution. If you need young play testers, consider offering a local elementary school teacher a brief talk in the classroom about designing games, followed by some game play. If you are creative enough to design a game, I am sure you can come up with new and creative ways to reach game players.

THE 3 TYPES OF PLAY TESTS

There are three reasons to play test: to find out whether your idea has merit, to refine the game, and to see whether your game can stand up to the rigors of heavy gaming. I treat them as three different types of play tests

Is It On Track – this can be done with a soft prototype of paper and pencil markings on cards and board. At this stage, you are looking to find out whether your concept basically works. Create enough components to bear this out. You may not need to enlist the help of other players to do this. Assume the roles of all the players yourself. If, after this step, you are still unsure, then recruit other players, but still keep the prototyping minimal. It is unwise to waste too much time and effort on perfecting graphics, when there is still so much room for change.

Fine Tuning – this can be the longest phase of the game's development. Play and replay your game until it flows smoothly from beginning to end and that it is actually a good game (see below in "What Makes a Good Game Good?"). In this phase, you may find that you have to drop certain game play elements, radically revise others and even add new elements. You are looking for balance; a game that is engaging from start to finish for everyone at the table. Testing groups should include the lower and higher age ranges you are targeting for your game, as well as a range in number of players. For example, if your game should work for 2–8 players, ages 10 and up, be sure you have tested it with a 10 year old and an adult, with 2 players and 8 players and all the numbers in between.

Breaking the Game – now that your game is nearing completion, write up a complete draft of the rules and hand the game and the rules to some experienced game players. Tell them you are testing for flaws in game play, that you are trying to 'break the game'. Ask them to try extreme strategies or purposely put themselves into unusual predicaments in the game to see how it holds up under these conditions. This is also a good place to give the game a hard test with the minimum and maximum number of players to see if any special problems arise from these extremes.

THE PERFECT PLAY TEST

There are three main elements to a great play test.

<u>Vary the Players</u> – plenty of play testing should take place for any of your game ideas, but using the same play testers repeatedly decreases the value of the feedback you receive. It is important to bring new players into your game, as they bring different points of views and experiences to the table, broadening the value and scope of the feedback.

<u>Stay Out of It</u> – a good designer is a good observer. It is better to watch a play test happen than to participate in it. First, it gives a better view of all the players. Notice how they interact, what their decision-making processes are, and if they are getting bored. This will help you identify problems with the interactivity, the complexity, and pacing of the game. When a problem arises with the game avoid the temptation to jump to the rescue. Ask the players, "How do you think we should handle this?" Players will usually choose the path that is most intuitive to them and it may not be what you had expected. If you like your solution best, tell them what it is and see what they think. If you are unsure, let them to play it their way. Whether their idea is better or worse, it is still information that helps you make the best choice.

<u>Sounds of Success</u> – I categorize the sounds of success as: oohs, aahs, guffaws, and applause. If you hear an 'ooh' while game testing, that means a player has discovered something they really like in the game play. Make a note of it and why it happened. Can you create more of these 'oohs'? If you hear 'aahs' while testing that usually means that a player now understands an aspect of the game that was previously unclear. This means you need to address something more clearly in the rules or in the explanation of the game, or it means that there is a strategy that unveils itself as the game develops, which is a good thing. If you hear 'guffaws', this is generally a good thing, unless your game is meant to be quite serious. Assuming the laughter is a good response, make a note of when

and why it happened, and see if you can inject more into the game. And, of course, if you get 'applause' or any type of kudos, this is a great compliment to your game, and you know you are on the right track.

WHAT MAKES A GOOD GAME GOOD?

I have identified 11 elements of a good game. They are mentioned here and detailed below (note: the initials reading down spell out 'down briefs'—there is nothing significant about that phrase but as a game guy, I had to make them spell something)...

Destiny Driven
Original & Fresh
Wait Time Minimal
Not Predictable
Broad Appeal
Replayable
Interactive
Equal Opportunity For All
Fun
Simple to Learn
… **M**onetarily Worth It

Destiny Driven – The players feel they have some control over the outcome of the game; that if they win, it had something to do with their decisions and skill. Games that are driven too much by luck lose their appeal after age 7 or 8.

Original & Fresh – most games are composed of bits and pieces of all the games that have come before. What is it about your game that sets it apart? A novel twist to a theme or an inventive use of game play will go a long way toward getting your game sold, both to a game company and a game consumer.

Wait Time Minimal – players do not like to wait too long between turns. Games with quick turn-taking or simultaneous play keep players engaged. Physical or mental activities that happen between turns, such as calculations, sorting, plotting and strategy choices, all help with player involvement. Try to avoid game play where players are eliminated early and become mere bystanders.

Not Predictable/Surprising – your game needs to offer something unexpected. Generally, the more moments of surprise, the better your game will be received. Randomizers such as dice or card can offer this unpredictability. When another player's action affects another player's choices, this adds a nice tension.

Broad Appeal – is your game topically appealing to a broad audience? Is it targeted at a wide enough age range and number of player? Aim for a broad target to maximize your chances for success.

Replayable – if you can craft a game players want to play again right after playing it once, you have a hit. A game that is played once and then put on the shelf for a year, is not going to become a best-seller. The replay-ability of a game is often influenced most by differing available strategies and skills that improve with repeat play. And generally, a little laughter aids in the desire to replay a game.

Interactive – offer players the chance to interact frequently, or you might as well be crafting a game of group solitaire. These can be cooperative, competitive or purely social moments, but they are necessary for keeping players involved.

Equal Opportunity & Winning Chances For All – going into a game, players want to feel they have a chance to win. Do not create a game that is imbalanced towards one certain skill set or knowledge set. It can turn players off. Likewise, players want to feel they have a chance to catch up if they end up behind at any point in the game. Design a catch-up feature to keep everyone in the game.

Fun – games intrinsically are meant to be fun. Fun can mean different things to different people; it does not necessarily mean players have to laugh. Steer clear of game concepts that can be intimidating, such as tough word games or trivia games on too narrow of a topic. Players will usually avoid game play that can make them look awkward, foolish or stupid.

Simple to Learn – players want to spend more time playing the game than learning it. A game that plays for 2–3 hours can be more involved to learn than a 30-minute party game. Make sure the length of the learning curve is rewarded commensurate with the depth of game play.

...Monetarily Worth It – this is an element that you may have little control over. Keep in mind that a game buyer looking at a game priced at $29.95, for example, has an expectation of how much that game will weigh before they pick it up. There is a 'heft value' directly associated with the cost of a game. Make sure your game price lives up to the components. *The Hobbit*, a game I co-designed, included 'gemstones' made of colored glass beads because they had good 'heft value'.

Rules Were Made to Be Broken

You may come up with a great game that fails in one or more of the elements above. Rest assured, there are games out there that have violated these 'good game tenets' and have gone on to sell millions. *How to Host a Murder* was specifically designed to be played only once, so it deliberately failed at being replayable. *Monopoly* had an extremely complicated rule book for its day, and was difficult to learn. In *Risk,* one player could be eliminated within 20 minutes and have to wait an hour for the game to finish. View the elements above as guidelines and not hard-and-fast rules. Be aware that you might need to 'break the rules' every now and again.

Game-Storming

Game-storming is brainstorming about games. Invariably, at some point, you will hit a mental roadblock; a place where you need to tweak your game but are stuck with no new ideas. This is a method I use to jumpstart my brain, a concept I borrowed and adapted from the Otis College of Art and Design. Keep in mind this is merely a process to get the creative juices flowing; it may not necessarily solve your problem. Follow the flow of ideas to see where they take you—you never know what great things may come of it!

The process has the acronym: S-C-A-M-P-E-R. Below are the details for what each letter stands for, with a practical application and example.

I recommend starting by writing a detailed sentence describing your game As an example, we will use the classic kids' game of *Jacks*.

> *Example: A children's game where you pick up an increasing number of small items in between bouncing a ball and catching it.*

S – Substitute

Substitution is replacing one element in your game with another. Using the example above, you would underline a few key words and play around with swapping them out with other words.

> *Example: A children's game where you pick up an increasing number of small items in between bouncing a ball and catching it.*

What if 'children's' became 'adult' and 'small items' became 'bottle caps'—then you might have 'Pub Jacks', a beer drinking game.

C – Combine

Combining is useful, not only for helping a game in mid-stage but, also for coming up with the beginning idea. The object is to bring two or more items together that would not normally be combined and see what ideas sprout. I create a spreadsheet of fun ideas, cool mechanics, and interesting items. Then I divide the list in two parts and put them side-by-side. Reading the random pairings always stimulates humorous, fun and unique ideas.

> *Example: One random pairing put Jacks with Spinning Tops.*

Imagine trying to grab jacks that are being knocked around by the top… an interesting twist on the more set version of the game.

A – Add

Look to increase an element in the game or add a new challenge to it.

> *Example A children's game (with 2 children simultaneously) picking up an increasing number*

of small items in between bouncing a ball (twice),
(running around in a circle) and catching it.

M – Modify

The term 'modify' used here means 're-theme'. A change in theme can turn a humdrum game into a knockout. While I was developing a game called Pecking Order, a bird-themed stacking game, another game was released using that name. In game-storming a new theme involving stacking, I visualized a totem pole. With this new tiki theme, the game really gelled. I incorporated some neat new game pieces sold the game, Tiki Topple, within a month. Using our Jacks example, you might 'modify' it as follows:

> *Example: A children's game where you pick up an*
> *increasing number of toy astronauts in between*
> *shooting a rocket and it falling to the ground.*

P – Put to Other Use

As you browse the aisles of your local art supply, hobby, hardware or educational store, be on the lookout for items that have play value, and can be repurposed for use in a game. Did you know Play-doh started as a wallpaper cleaner, and wax markers used in a chemical plant became Crayola crayons? The world is filled with items with play value just waiting to be discovered. Using our example, how might we use a set of chattering teeth?

> *Example: A children's game where you pick up an*
> *increasing number of small items while a pair of*
> *wind-up chattering teeth winds down.*

E – Eliminate

Too often, designers add too many elements to a game, trying to find the right balance. Sometimes it is necessary to step back and look at what can be simplified or taken away. Some of the best game play is elegantly simple. Eliminating elements also helps to identify what the core elements of the game are.

> *Example: A children's game where you pick up*
> *~~an increasing number of~~ small items in between*
> *bouncing a ball and catching it.*

R – Rearrange/Reverse

You can also reverse or otherwise rearrange the order in which the elements of a game are executed. One of the most successful TV game shows did this by taking the age-old standard of asking a Question and getting an Answer. Jeopardy, brilliantly and simply, give the Answer first, then asked for the Question?

> *Example: A children's game where you pick up an*
> *increasing number of small items and then bounce*
> *a ball and catch it.*

OVERHAULING GAME MECHANICS

There are two reasons you might perform a complete overhaul of your game.

The first is when, usually early on in the design, you discover what you have imagined just does not work. There may be very little to salvage from this concept, and so you decide to start over.

Another reason to do an overhaul would be if after you have tweaked your game repeatedly, you still have not found the right balance. Sometimes the best approach is to throw everything out the window (temporarily), and try a completely different approach to the game. By doing this, you gain a whole new perspective on your game, what works, what doesn't, and gives you more insight to what you might try next. This complete redesign does not need to be well thought out or even practical. It needs to give you a different angle of approach. I know one designer who, when stuck on a game that is not coming together properly, takes his board game and tries to build a card game out of it. Often it is the element of breaking completely free of your old mind-set that gives you the insight needed to re-approach the old game and take it to completion.

WHEN IS IT ENOUGH?

We designers rarely ever feel 100% finished with our designs. So, how do you decide when you have taken your game far enough?

I recommend using the 11 elements of a good game, mentioned above, to gauge when your level of completion is enough. For each element, give your game a number or letter grade… or better yet, get others to give your game a grade. The grading helps you determine which areas of the game need more work, and also gives you an overall grade point average for your game. I use a letter grade of B+ as a minimum benchmark. If my game has not hit that level overall, then it is not ready to send out. You can set your sights higher or lower, it is your choice. Remember, as a licensor, you will have to draw the line somewhere and send your baby off into the unbiased hands of game companies to be scrutinized and dissected, so make sure you are comfortable with the development grade that you have chosen. Ultimately, you cannot make any money, until your game is completed—you cannot win if you do not play.

You can continue to make minor changes to your game after you send it out, but make sure companies reviewing it are using the current rules and components.

Writing Rules Right

I rarely write any rules before I move into the 'break the game' play test mode. Usually there is an endless array of tweaks in the game play that would mean endless rewrites of the rules. I recommend not writing the rules until you need to do so.

The following are my guidelines for writing rules, adapted from guidelines, Michael Gray, Sr. Director of New Product Acquisition at Hasbro, has presented at industry workshops.

Rules Guidelines

Rules Draft Date – update your file name every time you make a change. Keep all the old drafts. You never know when you will want to revisit something you tried earlier, and you might not remember quite how you did it. It is handy to have your earlier drafts to refer back to.

Game Name and Tag Line – the more catchy and clever the better.

Side Panel Specs – this covers the number of players, age ranges, time to learn and duration of play.

Contents – a list of all the components of the game and their quantities. Note: side panel specs and contents can be omitted on the rule sheet, if they are included on a separate 'Spec Sheet' outlined in the chapter on Submissions.

Overview/Intro (optional) – this is a short blurb on what the game is about. This is not necessary for all games. If there is a back story and some historical event that sets the stage for your game, this is where it goes.

Assembly (if required) – this covers things that you have to do once before play, such as put together an item or apply labels. This is where the directions for setting up the game of *Mousetrap* would go, for example.

Object of the Game – outline succinctly what it takes to win the game. This gives players a framework to keep in the back of their mind while they read on.

Rules – Rules are the Bible of the game and will be referred to when players are seekng clarification on game play. Make your writing style clear and concise. You can include graphics to aid in describing complicated concepts, but do not bury a key rule in the caption under the picture. List the rules in a logical sequence and avoid reference to future rules. If a rule has an exception, follow up with it directly in a Note; it might get missed if you insert it somewhere else in the rules. The Rules contain the following four segments.

Set Up – list the things players must to do every time before beginning play.

Basic Play – explain everything about playing the game. Within this section, highlight important terms, and include details of special components such as cards, dice and spaces on the board. If your game is complicated, include at the start of the Basic Play, a short, bulleted list of the elements that happen each turn, often called 'turn order'.

Scoring – detail how players earn points.

Winning – describe the condition for winning the game. This must be a concrete outcome or score. If it is possible for a game to end in a tie, include a solution for ending a tie-break.

Strategy Hints (as needed) – usually these are only needed for games of significant depth. Michael Gray, from Hasbro, makes the observation that including strategy hints can be a perk for the reader. They may or may not choose to keep the hints to themselves; that is their bonus for reading the rules.

Variant Rules (as needed) – you may have suggestions for a more advanced game that can be outlined here, or special rules for playing solitaire.

Whatever the variations may be, they belong at the end of the rules.

Special Thanks (optional) – if you have play testers or friend and family that need thanking, do it here. It will be up to the manufacturer to decide whether they will be included in the published game.

Contact Info – include your name and contact info. For licensors/designers this can simply be an email or phone number along with your name. For self-publishers, list how you would prefer customers to contact you. such as, "For issues concerning the rules or for more information on any of our games, contact us at customerservice@greatgames.com, or by mail at 1234 Boardgame Blvd, Playwith, ME 01234."

Self-Publishing

THE 3 P's

Although there are many facets to running a business, I will only be addressing those areas specific to the game industry. To begin, there are 3 P's essential to your game's success: Placement, Packaging, and Pricing.

PLACEMENT

Let's look again at the industry overview. The trickiest part for those in the role of game publisher is getting their games in the hand of the retail buyers and getting them to say, 'yes' to putting them on the shelf. Early in the book I mentioned two areas that are often not given enough attention by start up companies; Sales and Packaging. Let's address Sales.

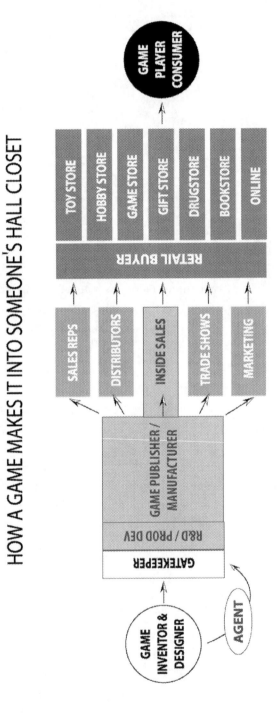

GAME INDUSTRY OVERVIEW:
HOW A GAME MAKES IT INTO SOMEONE'S HALL CLOSET

GAME INVENTOR & DESIGNER

AGENT

GATEKEEPER

R&D / PROD DEV

GAME PUBLISHER / MANUFACTURER

SALES REPS

DISTRIBUTORS

INSIDE SALES

TRADE SHOWS

MARKETING

RETAIL BUYER

TOY STORE

HOBBY STORE

GAME STORE

GIFT STORE

DRUGSTORE

BOOKSTORE

ONLINE

GAME PLAYER CONSUMER

It is imperative that you get your game in front of as many game buyers as possible. Here are some key ways to reach the all-important buyers:

Sales Reps – these are independent sales people or sales teams that usually represent several related lines and call on accounts in a specific territory. They earn a percentage of sales dollars by doing the traveling, pitching the product, and taking orders. The accounts they set up are the customers you ship to and bill. It can be challenging to find reps that will be successful with your game(s). Reps are generally most successful with, and put most of their focus on the products that are easiest to sell. It is important to support reps throughout the selling process to help your chances of success. Good reps are worth their weight in gold, because they act on your behalf to get your games in front of buyers, keep up with accounts spread out across the region, and they are not on your payroll!

Distributors – they buy directly from you at a significant discount, usually 25–35% off of wholesale, so they can sell to their own account base—who they ship to and bill. The discount becomes their mark up; they sell at your list wholesale price. The plus side is they buy larger quantities up front and you do not have to worry about account management. The flip side of that is you may never know what stores are carrying and re-ordering your game. As with sales reps, they are working on your behalf, while creating no additional overhead costs, i.e. not on your payroll.

Inside Sales – this is a person or team hired by you to handle the sales of your products. Their duties can vary but generally they handle the big sales accounts directly as well as manage any sales reps and distributors. They are also responsible for coordinating and managing the trade shows you attend, both consumer and industry shows. Chances are, especially when you are starting up your company, this person/team will have other duties as well. It could be you—running the daily operations and handling sales. Whoever it is, make sure they are excellent at sales. It is too important a job to settle for less, and their performance can make or break your business.

Trade Shows – these fall into two categories; consumer shows and industry, or trade-only, shows. Consumer shows are where the end customers—the game players—attend. You can sell your game at full retail price, usually selling 1 or 2 at a time. Trade-only shows are for retail buyers. You are selling at wholesale price to mom and pop specialty stores usually in quantities of a half dozen to two dozen. There will also be chain stores, such as Barnes & Noble and Borders, where you are hoping to write larger orders, usually at some negotiated discount price. The objective is to write orders at these shows, but often you will have a lot of follow up to do afterwards to make the sales final.

Marketing – this is a broad umbrella and can cover everything from a postcard mailer to a fully-developed, direct-to-consumer website. You decide what avenues to pursue to increase awareness of your company, your games and getting them in the hands of retail buyers and the game player.

Looking beyond these channels of distribution, consider other non-traditional selling venues. *Cranium* is a great example of this. They were able to strike a deal with Starbucks. During the good-weather months, the *Cranium* crew would host 'patio parties' at Starbucks, teaching and playing their game which was for sale inside the store. Games had never been sold in a coffeehouse before, and it was a huge marketing success.

PACKAGING

Let's say that you have your great-playing game in the hands of a retail buyer, now what? How do they decide which of the hundreds of games they look at, will go on their shelves? Yes, the game play has to be fun, but just as important, the concept of the game must be appealing to their customers and the packaging must convey what is inside cleanly, concisely and attractively. The bottom line is that the game is going to be sitting on a shelf or pictured on a computer screen and it will be expected to sell itself. The packaging is so important that unless you are a package designer by trade, you should not rely on your own judgment to produce a good game box.

Whether you are designing it yourself, or hiring a packaging designer, here are a few things to consider:

First, many stores have modular shelving, which means the distance between shelves is usually 12 inches. The box height should not be much over 10.5 inches, allowing about a 2-inch clearance at the top. This makes it easy for a customer to reach above the box and grab it. A 10.5" x 10.5" is considered the standard accepted maximum box size.

Considering the different ways a box might end up on the shelf, makes the depth of the box also important. A box without much depth stands the risk of falling when placed standing up on its side. Usually a 2.5"–3" box depth works well for this reason, and gives you better presence when the game is displayed laying down flat.

It is tempting to create a box that is an unusual shape to help it stand out on the shelves, among the other games, but this can also be the reason your game is turned down by a retail buyer. The shelf and floor space of the retail environment is called 'real estate' because every inch is considered to be a money-making opportunity. If your odd-sized or odd-shaped box wastes space on the shelf or is hard to display, a retail buyer may relegate it to an out-of-the-way spot in the store, or simply choose to not bring it in. There is no place on modern day retail shelves for the old Monopoly-sized box because nowadays you can fit 2 or 3 games in the same amount of space.

Proper weight distribution inside the box is also important to keep it from toppling over when displayed. Keep this in mind when designing the cardboard dividers or plastic-molded inserts in the box that compartmentalize the components.

The inexperienced package designer often tries to fit too much information on the front of the box. The front is used to entice a customer to pick it up: so keep it clean, simple, and attractive. Too much clutter looks sloppy and sends a confusing message to the potential buyer. Put all your 'selling' copy on the back of the box. Do not cut corners by printing a black and white or two-color box front. You rarely get second chances to grab the interest of the consumer. If you are severely under cost restraints, a black and white or two-color box back is an option to consider.

It is good practice to take your packaging mock-up into a store (with their permission, of course) and see what it looks like on the shelf, before you go to press. Against the kaleidoscope of other games, does yours stand out? Do you like what you see?

PRICING

The game industry is considered a 'keystone' industry in terms of price markups. This means you would normally take your production costs, double it to get your wholesale price and double that again to get your suggested retail price.

Use this formula to work backwards as well. If you have a big box party game that you think should sell in retail stores at $29.95, stores would expect a wholesale price not more than $15, so your manufacturing costs better come in at $7.50 or less.

COST x 2 = WHSLE
WHSLE x 2 = RETAIL

RETAIL ÷ 2 = WHSLE
WHSLE ÷ 2 = COST

The hobby market expects components to be of a higher-grade, so it is more accepting of a game that runs a little higher in retail price than the average specialty or mass market game. In the hobby market you might see complex games with a lot of components sell for as much as $60. Just make sure that the game play, along with the components, warrant that higher price.

In the specialty market, a party game can run for as much as $30. Ideally this market prefers games that come in at $25 or $20. For the mass market, $20 would be the high end.

There are always exceptions to these rules but it is generally unwise to stray too far from the norm.

TIME IS OF THE ESSENCE

Having cash is important, but timing your cash flow is as important. The 4th Quarter is by far when the most of sales are made. At The Game Keeper, sales in November and December made up 80% of our sales for the entire year. This means that the other ten months, on average, resulted in just 2% per month. When planning your manufacturing timetable, you can delay production of your games until mid-year. If you ship games by the beginning of September, that gives you time to get the games into stores, in time to see if there will be sell-through, and get more substantial holiday orders placed as a result. This way the money you pay out for production will spend less time inactive, and you will see significant returns much quicker than you would if you produced the game too early.

You can go to trade shows with a mock-up of your game that is near production quality, take pre-orders on your games and see what kind of interest you generate. More and more established game companies do this with several games, and go into production only with the games that garner sufficient orders.

SKILLS FOR THE SELF-PUBLISHER

In an earlier chapter, I detailed the skill set required of the designer. Now, for the self-publisher, we will be adding another list of skills on top of that.

Venture Capitalist – it takes money to make money. The one cost that is a given is the cost of printing games. The most economic starting print run number is 5,000 games. At that quantity, you are getting a production cost that works for keystone markups. In the hobby market, I hear of companies running smaller quantities, which does work for some, but they often have to settle for smaller markups to bring their retail price in line with where it needs to be for the retailer. Beyond the costs of designing and printing the game, you need to be prepared financially to stick around. It takes a game 3-years to hit its stride in most cases. Can you last that long, taking into account the big cost of trade shows, travel and marketing? Do not forget to add the day-to-day expenditures of operating a small business, such as office supplies, utilities, etc.

Another benefit of running 5,000 games is you have a better read on the sell-through of your game and whether it is building momentum. By the time your warehouse is nearly cleaned out, you should know whether to invest in another run of 5,000 or possibly make a larger run. By running a small quantity, you will not have an accurate picture of how well your game is doing when you sell through your inventory. If you sell through the 2,000 games you produced, do you run another 2,000 at the lower price margin, or can you increase to 5,000? Obviously there are trade-offs given your confidence, acceptable risk, and available start up money. By drawing up a long-term, well-thought out financial plan and budget accordingly, you have a head start on moving forward with the best possible vision.

Market Analyst – be aware of what is going on in the market. Is the market hungry for your type of game? My first published trivia game released to rave reviews. Several months later, the *Who Wants To Be A Millionaire* board game came out and crushed sales of all trivia-based games. It had nothing to do with how good my trivia game was or anyone else's, timing was not in our favor.

Production Specialist – can you get the best price for your game to maximize your profit potential? Take the time necessary to figure out how to produce your game at the best quality for the best price. It may be tempting to think you can order all the pieces—the board, the cards, the pawns, the dice, etc.—separately and then assemble them yourself to get the best price. Remember time is money and time, as well as money, must be spent wisely.

Warehouse Manager – be prepared for when that first truckload of games arrives. Do you have the space to store and prepare them for shipping? If you are not good at shipping games out, you are not going to make much money.

Bookkeeper – you have to be detail oriented and organized about keeping receipts, paying bills, and invoicing customers. Set up your books so when tax time comes around, you do not have to scramble and search to get things together. Also, are you informed and prepared to deal with commissions and royalties?

Account Manager – you will be coordinating shipping, billing, discounts, extended dating, and, inevitably, dealing with delinquent accounts.

Marketing Director – are you continuing to promote your products throughout the year, most importantly, at fourth quarter? Are you establishing your company as a brand? Do you have a plan in place to promote future releases?

<u>National Sales Manager</u> – yes, you will have to travel. Can you persuade people that your game is better than all the others? Can you motivate sales people to do the same?

If you are ready and able to juggle all these hats and more, you have a fighting chance to become a successful self-publisher.

As a closing note about self-publishing, I want to add, that while it may be an all-consuming job, it is in my opinion, the best industry there is. Every day, hopefully, you will go to work at a job that you truly love. I have made a lot of lifelong friends in this field because the people in it are genuinely nice. There is a tremendous sense of camaraderie here that I have not experienced in any other industry. While the job may be challenging, the personal rewards, will go far beyond all the good money you can earn.

Licensing

Two Definitions

There are two different uses for the word 'licensing' in the game and toy industry.

The first definition refers to a game that is tied to a particular recognizable 'licensed property' or branded entity. For instance, *Simpsons' Clue* or the *Deal or No Deal* board game are examples of games tied to a license. While the *Simpsons* and *Deal or No Deal* are two TV licensing entities, these popular brands can come from anywhere: film, music, fashion, pop culture, etc. Any household name has the potential to become a licensed property, lending its image recognition to games, clothing, toys, electronics, etc. The game manufacturer pays the owners of the property a licensing fee for use of their name, image and graphics to promote the product. If you develop a game that gets tied to a license, you will receive a smaller royalty percentage because the property will also be getting a slice. However, because your game now has name recognition, you stand to make more overall due to an increased quantity of games sold as a result of that name recognition.

The second definition pertains specifically to those game designers who assign the rights of their game concept to a game company in exchange for monetary compensation. This is the 'licensing' term we will continue to explore in this chapter.

What Companies Are Looking For

When asked what they are looking for, the people who review games for game companies will usually say, "I'll know it when I see it" or "Something with the WOW factor." Based on those comments, it may seem that designing games is like taking a shot in the dark. Here are a few tips to help you zero in on the target.

When others say that to be creative you have to think outside the box, I say the challenge is to be completely creative inside the box. Coming up with something radically innovative is not necessarily what these companies are looking for. If an idea has no precedents, it will be harder to market and customers will usually not take the time to puzzle it out. I have had the most success with games that are innovative, combined with something familiar. Chances are that if you can describe your game in one sentence, run 10-seconds of a video, or show a few photos, and the other person gets what the game is about, you have struck that familiar chord. And if you can see they get it and have an 'a-ha!' moment, then you probably have created a game that has innovation. It is up to you to provide the inspiration that uses something familiar and takes it one step further. This innovation can be unique game pieces, a creative theme, a new bit of game play, or all of the above. You are only limited by your imagination.

Complete, radical innovation does show up on the shelves from time to time, and is usually launched by start up companies. When it works, it means BIG business. These games often create new game categories, start trends and buck the 'business as usual' trend. Some of the rule breakers and category makers include:

Magic: The Gathering – the first collectible card game, hatched by Wizards of the Coast, a company working out of their garage at the time

Dungeons & Dragons – the brainchild of TSR founders, which initiated the role-playing genre

Scene It – which began the DVD game craze and was self-published after the inventor was turned down by several companies

How To Host a Murder – dinner party mystery games, designed to be played only once, were introduced by new game company, Decipher.

STANDING OUT

If a company is looking at hundreds, if not thousands, of games each year, how do you stand out? The best way is to design good games. Someone who has one published game, might be lucky, but someone who has half a dozen published games is a designer. The other traits that will make you memorable is being professional and easy to deal with. This will place you well above the majority of casual inventors.

Over time, as you walk the aisles at trade shows, make scheduled and impromptu meetings, and join in networking gatherings, you will find there is no shortage of information to be gleaned. Continue to evolve and educate yourself as a designer and you will become a desirable commodity. Being an informed designer puts you in an elite group.

TRADE SHOW ETIQUETTE

Trade shows are a great place to do business as a game designer. A lot of games, game companies, and industry people are gathered in one place; it can be like being a kid in a candy store. Despite the numerous distractions, keep in mind your purpose there—and that is 3-fold. First, you are pitching your game. Most will be at meetings that you have set up beforehand, but may include meetings that are impromptu. Second, you are being introduced to the 'gatekeepers' or other industry professionals who can help you get your game licensed. Third, you are seeing the new games that are being released to try to spot any trends and become familiar with the product lines of the companies with whom you are or will be dealing.

Remember, that the companies at the show, whether you have meetings set up with them or not, are there primarily to sell their games. Meetings with inventors to find new product is a secondary benefit to them. This means the retail buyers visiting the booths have first priority always! When you are in the booths, do not block the pathways or any product if possible. If you experience a cold shoulder from the staff in a booth, cut them some slack. They are under tremendous pressure to bring in orders and some tunnel vision towards buyers is to be expected. This means you may not even get access to some booths because you do not have an appointment and you are not a buyer. Keep the game company's perspective in mind at the shows and everyone will benefit.

Submissions

DISCLAIMER: when it comes to legal matters, it is best to consult a lawyer. This section is not meant to offer counsel, but merely to offer insight from one person's experience. If you have any doubt, or additional questions, please purse professional legal advice.

PROTECTING YOURSELF: THE ABC'S OF ©'S, TM'S & ®'S, NDA'S, AND PATPEND'S

Undoubtedly, the most frequently asked question from beginning inventors is "How Do I Protect My Game From Being Stolen?" How to best protect your idea is really a question for a lawyer, but I can offer some anecdotal information on what has worked for me. I cannot guarantee you will have the same positive outcomes as I have had, but the section below will give you some good information to help you make an informed decision on how to proceed in this area.

My overall view on copyrights and other forms of protection for a game is that it is very difficult to stop your game from being copied. That being said, it is probably something that you need not worry about. Now before you call your lawyer or send a doctor from the loony bin after me, let me explain exactly what I mean.

You can copyright your game, trademark certain elements and even hold a patent for it, but in reality, someone can make some very minor adjustments to your game concept and publish it. This is very hard to fight in court.

Let's ask ourselves another question, "Why would someone steal your game?" You may believe you have invented the hottest game in the last decade, but how do you know? How would anyone know? A thousand great-playing games are released each year and only a handful sell a significant number. The designers who created them and the game companies that published them all thought they were good, but no one can second guess the fickle game buyer as to what will be *hot*. Where is the motivation to steal an idea that is unproven with no guarantee of success? There is none.

Another reason your game is unlikely to be stolen is because of the quantity of games each year designed by independent game designers—we are the lifeblood of the industry. If your idea is really great, it is in the best interest of the game company to pay you fairly for your design to encourage you to bring them all your great ideas. Alienating you is counterproductive to their goal; to get great games to market year after year.

To help put your mind at ease, here is the scoop on the various methods of protecting your idea:

<u>Copyrights</u> – this is the simplest, least expensive, and easiest way to protect your game. Copyrights actually exist at the time of creation, but to legally uphold or contest a copyright, it first must by registered. That is were the Library of Congress comes in. By going to their website, www.copyright.gov, you can download the forms and instructions for obtaining a registered copyright for your game. The copyright is designed to protect your work of authorship (expression of your idea) in all textual

details. It is as simple as taking a copy of your game, filling out form TX, and sending them in with your filing fee, currently $45. Form TX protects the textual elements of your game, such as box copy and rules. If your game is an artistic rendition of an already established game, such as a cribbage board in the shape of a rocket, you can use form VA that protects the visual elements of your game. Copyright generally lasts for the lifetime of the author plus an additional 70 years. It does not matter to me whether it is the game publisher or me who files for copyright. Because I have not been challenged to uphold any copyrights, I cannot personally attest to how copyright laws and processes pan out in court.

Trademarks – these are used to protect a specific trademark or service mark; game names fall under 'trademark'. With a trademark you are protecting a specific name, tag line, and its look, used in a specific category (International Class = IC). The first step would be to go to the U.S. Patent and Trademark Office on-line, www.uspto.gov, and search on TESS to see if there is anything currently registered using your anticipated game name within category IC28 (Toys & Sporting Goods). This search is pretty comprehensive, but if you want to be 100% certain, it is best to hire a copyright attorney to do a formal search.

Unless your game's name is absolutely the only possible name for your game, I suggest you wait until the game is published before filing for trademark. I have had game names change before going to press. Even a slight modification could render a previously filed trademark registration pointless. The next step is to electronically file for your trademark using the USPTO website, showing first use in commerce, i.e. when it first shipped to a store, and pay the $325 fee. If you do not file electronically, the fee increases to $375. If your game falls into more than just the IC28 category, you must pay the same registration amount for each IC you want covered. If you do pre-register your trademark with an Intent to Use (ITU) application, i.e. before it is actually published, then you must file a Statement of Use (SOU) within 6 months of release and pay an additional $100. Trademarks last for 5 years automatically and then you file for continued use between years 5 and 6 and again just before the 10th year to extend the trademark. Once you have filed and received your physical registration certificate, you may switch from the TM to the ®. This filing process is a little bit trickier so read over the instructions online to determine whether you are comfortable filing yourself or prefer to hire a trademark lawyer. Again, it does not matter too much to me whether I hold the trademark or the game publisher does. This fee is more costly so usually I prefer that the publisher take care of it.

Patents – for a game, you would be applying for a utility patent as opposed to a design patent. The application process is VERY complex and correct wording is essential. I wholeheartedly recommend, if you decide to apply for a patent, that you use a patent attorney to minimize the risk of the patent not adequately protecting your game. The patent process is a very costly one so make sure your game is so completely original that it is worth patenting. You can also file a Provisional Patent, which is more nominal in cost, and gives you a period of one year, to file for a formal, Non-Provisional Patent. This way you can test the waters to see if your idea will fly and truly has the need for a patent.

I have never filed for a patent and have always questioned their importance in the gaming world. For example, imagine Wizards of the Coast with their patent for *Magic: The Gathering*. When Decipher was first to follow with their collectible card game, *Star Trek: The Next Generation*, would Wizards choose to take Decipher to court and try to uphold their patent, consuming time and money with no absolute guarantee they would win? Or should they allow Decipher to continue with their CCG and hope that the *Star Trek: TNG* game would serve to broaden the base of card players who, over time, might gravitate over to *Magic: TG*. This is in fact, how Wizards approached it. Ultimately, the question is not whether you should obtain a patent, but what would you do with your patent if you had one?

Non-Disclosure Agreements (NDA's) – both the game designer and the game publisher can use these documents to protect themselves. The documents can be titled differently from one user to another. One popular tag is that 'Confidentiality Agreement'. The purpose of these documents is to protect one entity when showing or being shown ideas from another entity.

As a game designer, I have a standard non-disclosure agreement, and I have only used it once. It seems almost pointless to ask a company to 'not steal my idea'. It is not in any company's best interest to steal an idea. They are always looking to develop new relationships with promising game designers.

Game companies feel the reverse need for protection: that you will not sue them if they come up with a game that has some similarities to yours. Let's face it, a company that looks at hundreds and hundreds of game ideas each year likely has seen a game, and possibly has one in the works, with the same theme as yours, with basic components similar to yours, and/or with game play that matches yours. They are looking to protect themselves from these inevitable coincidences and the inventor who might take them to court.

If you show your game to the largest game companies, they will not sign your non-disclosure document and will insist you sign theirs. That is the nature of the business, and you will have to be okay with it if you want to play with the 'big boys'.

THE SPEC SHEET

This could be the one most important document that gets your game idea viewed and given careful consideration. It can alternately be called a 'one sheet' or 'b-sheet'; the title I prefer is 'spec sheet'.

A spec sheet is a one-page flyer that covers all the details of your game in a quick-to-read format for the 'gatekeepers' at the game companies. Because this one page can give them all the information they need to make their decision to review your game further or to pass, it has become a popular tool for communicating with the busy game manufacturer.

<u>Overview/Intro</u> – an optional few sentences about your game especially if there is a back story or some historical event that sets the stage for the game.

<u>Objective</u> – an outline of what it takes to win the game.

<u>Brief Synopsis of Play</u> – in one paragraph, give the flavor of what a basic turn looks like so the reader can see the level of strategy and luck involved. If there are different stages, outline them. Put in any elements that make your game unique, but leave out or abbreviate all the elements that are standard for most games.

<u>Notes</u> – this is where you can mention other variations you may have, any unique marketing ideas, any special features and benefits, etc.

<u>Prototype Status</u> – state that you have a 'complete prototype' if you have nothing more to add to it, but if, for instance you are supplying 100 out of the 500 cards needed for a complete game, mention it here.

<u>Contact Info</u> – this is important. Do not forget it!

TOPPLIN' TIKIS

The Heads Up Tiki Game of Totem Domination!

# of Players: 2-4 players
Age Range: 8 and up
Start Playing In: 3 minutes
Game Length: 15-25 minutes

Game Components:
- 9 Tikis
- 27 Totem Scoring Cards
- 28 Action cards (7 each in 4 colors)
- 4 Scoring Tokens
- 1 Scoring Board

Object:
To gain the most points using your Action cards to move tikis up, drop them down, or just plain eliminate them in an attempt to place the tikis matching your Totem Scoring card in the correct position on the totem pole.

Basic Game:
The 9 Tiki tokens are placed randomly one on top of the other for form the totem pole. Each player draws a Totem Scoring card which determines which 3 tikis can score for them this round and the position they must be in to score. Each player then takes their identical hand of 6 cards (7 cards in a two-player game). The Action cards allow basic moves such as moving a tiki up 1, 2, or 3 spaces, or dropping any tiki to the bottom, or eliminating the bottom tiki on the totem pole.
Players alternate using their action cards. As the totem gets shorter and shorter, players frantically try to jockey their scoring tikis into scoring position. When there are only 3 tikis left in the totem pole, the round ends and scoring begins. Players score according to Totem Scoring cards, points are tallied, and a new round begins as before. At the end of a scoring round, if any player has passed the '25 points' mark, the game ends with the player the furthest ahead winning and being named the Top Totem Tiki Chief.

Note:
- The 9 Tiki tokens should be 3 molded pieces for the most satisfying game experience, but can be scaled down and replaced by cards and the board changed to a scoring pad.
- GameWright is has license for this game in U.S.-speaking countries, schedule for release 2007.

Game Development Stage: Completed prototype

1234 Game St • Playwith, ME 01234 • ph: 123-456-7890 • email: me@greatgames.com

FINDING COMPANIES

Armed with a comprehensive spec sheet, how do you find the companies most likely to publish your game? One of the simplest methods is to go into a game store and look at the products that have some similarity to yours, i.e. a silly party game, a light strategy family game, etc. Pick up those boxes and check to see who the company is and make note of the address, city, website, or other contact info listed. You can also do the same through many retail game websites, however, not all will list a game's manufacturer.

Visit the websites of the specific game companies you are interested in contacting to get a better feel of their product line and how your game fits into it. Make notes on the games from these companies, as well as email contact info listed and their physical address.

A couple of other websites that can be helpful in finding websites of game companies are my website, www.gamedesigncentral.com, and www.boardgamegeek.com.

Do not rush into the query phase before doing this background work! It is essential that your game fits within a company's line of games; for instance, sending an adult party game to a children's game company is a waste of everyone's time. It is also important you sound like a pro when you contact these businesses. Being able to talk to a company about their line and showing you understand how your game fits within it will go a long way to getting an attentive reception.

THE DO'S AND DON'TS OF THE QUERY

Your query and follow up letters, sent via email or snail mail, are your first step to getting your game reviewed by a company, so you want to appear professional and knowledgeable. Do not send up any 'red flags' that indicate you may be difficult to deal with or need a lot of hand-holding. Keep the query short, simple and to the point. The goal is to get them interested, not to give them your life story.

The typical progression of the submission process is…

1. Send an email to the address you have, such as customerservice@ greatgames.com or info@greatgames.com. Ask whether they accept

outside submissions and for the contact information for the person in charge of reviewing submissions.

2. Once you have the contact information, send a brief email to that person stating that you have a game you would like to submit, and ask for details on their submission process. Let them know you have a 1-page spec sheet with all the details of your game you can email them.

3. If you do not hear anything in two weeks, try again. You can try one more time if necessary, and if you do not get a response, it is probably best to move on to other prospects.

4. If they say 'yes', follow their instructions for submissions. It may be that you send the spec sheet only, or the spec sheet with rules, or you may be asked to send them the prototype. Include the spec sheet and rules, as well as a follow up letter stating you are sending these elements per request, and add a few other sentences to make it personal and convey your enthusiasm for what you have created.

Both the query letter and follow up letter are representations of who you are. Below are some recommended Do's and Don'ts to help you put your best foot forward:

> DON'T get too cutesy, even though you are dealing with games that are playful in nature. The more business-like you are, the more competent you sound.

> DON'T mention anything about money or contracts in this letter. There will be plenty of time for that discussion should they show interest in licensing your game.

> DON'T mention other companies who may have reviewed the game or to whom you are sending it. Give them your full attention and they will give you theirs.

> DO mention your credentials if you have some: other published games, other game work you have done, or skills that enhance the status of your game. For instance, if your game is a baseball game for kids and you are a Little League coach, or a teacher with an educational game, then briefly mention that.

DO mention the positive results of any objective play testing you have done. Play tests with friends and family are not objective. Do not simply say that 'they liked it' but use the positive results to highlight a specific aspect of the game, e.g. "The play testers loved the challenge of balancing peanuts on their nose."

DO know who they are and demonstrate this knowledge in your communications, i.e. Mention one of their products and say, "I believe that my card game, *Twinkle Star*, fits nicely in with your line of card games, in particular, it has a laugh-out-loud aspect similar to your game, *Teensy-Weensy*."

DON'T give them deadlines. Most of these 'gatekeepers' have other roles they fill within the company and we designers have no idea what deadlines they are already facing. Tell them you will check in with them in 2–4 weeks. Follow up in that specified time, but do not pressure them into a 'yes' or 'no' answer. Say that you wanted to make sure they had received the query from earlier, and re-state the query, saying you will follow up later.

DON'T offer to make changes right off the bat. That sends the signal that you think your game is weak. You should, however, be open to making changes should a company request it.

DON'T ask them to sign a non-disclosure agreement as most companies will not sign one anyway. By asking them what their submission process is, you have left them the opportunity to ask you to sign their agreement before sending in a submission.

DON'T use the 5 phrases that are dead-giveaways that you are inexperienced, detailed below.

THE TOP 5 PHRASES TO **NEVER** USE

When I worked for a small game company reviewing game submissions, I could easily identify the inexperienced inventor when they would use one of the following lines. Usually, the less said, the better. Avoiding these phrases will increase your chances of getting serious consideration for your game. If you are drafting an introductory email, sending a cover letter, or looking to make phone contact, do not say,...

5. *"This game will be the next Monopoly."*

This proves that you really have no idea the huge success of Monopoly. Monopoly has transcended being simply a very successful game; it has achieved the status of a phenomenon. You may know you can buy a Monopoly game based on your favorite city or football team but did you know you can also get Monopoly themed with Harley Davidson's, US National Parks, Bass Fishing, and Elvis? It is truly amazing, and no game will ever duplicate the success of Monopoly, much less surpass it.

While you are at it, avoid comparisons to other mega hits such as Trivial Pursuit, Clue, Battleship, etc.

4. *"This game will sell (or make us) millions."*

This proves you do not know how cash flows in this industry and you have unrealistically high expectations for your game. There are so many elements that have to be in alignment for a game to sell a million copies or make a million dollars, which include but are not limited to; the public has to be ready for it, packaging has to be just right, pricing has to fit with the current economy, the name and tag line have to strike a chord with buyers, the theme must have mass appeal, the game play must be innovative, etc.

Most medium and small game companies consider it a success to have a game that sells 20,000 to 30,000 copies a year, for several years in a row. Even seasoned industry pros cannot accurately predict a mega-hit, although they try. So how can you—someone new to the industry—have such great insight? A comment such as this only serves to make you sound like a newbie, or worse, foolish.

3. "How can I be sure you won't steal my idea?"

I have seen this phrased any number of ways but at its core it still means one thing, "I am paranoid and hard to deal with". This sends up a red flag that you will need to be educated about the industry and you will likely be a problem (and so it will be easier to avoid dealing with you altogether).

2. "My game is highly educational."

This is not necessarily a bad phrase to use, and in fact, can be a good phrase if it is true and you are contacting a company that publishes educational games. However, way too often beginning game designers, looking to describe their game in the best possible light will use this phrase even when their game has very little educational value. If you are going to use this phrase, you have to be able to back it up with details and facts!

I have seen the word 'educational' used for games whose educational value was solely that you rolled the die and then 'counted' that many spaces to move your pawn. I have also seen it used for 'color-matching' where you put your pawn on the start space that matches your color pawn; for 'problem-solving' where you had to choose to take the route to the right or left; and for "addition" where you were simply adding your two dice rolls together.

Educational value is very important and is becoming more and more important to companies that are not necessarily considered educational game companies. If your game works with current curricular standards and lesson plans, then do mention that your game is 'educational'.

1. "I've played it with all my friends and family and they love it."

Seemingly harmless enough, this phrase has 3 distinct problems.

One, since it has been and will be used by at least 98% of beginning inventors this phrase has become a cliché, and as such is seen to be almost totally meaningless. Two, of course your friends and family love it... that is why they are your friends and family. They love you and everything you do, so why wouldn't they love your game? What a game company really wants to know is how it was received by nonpartisan play test groups. And three, the fact that you mention testing it with friends and family by default means you have not tested it with anyone else: and this would be a serious flaw in the design process. The more play testing you do with different groups, the better feedback you get and the more potential design errors you will avoid.

So don't use this or any of the 5phrases above. They are a sure sign that you are green when it comes to creating games!

Pitching In-Person

If there is a trade show on the horizon and it is one you can attend with game in hand, make email queries ahead of time to schedule meetings with the companies on your list. There is no better way to convey your enthusiasm for your game than by making the presentation yourself. Your success in getting appointments will likely differ from company to company due to their schedules during the show and other factors. Consider yourself lucky if you get a half dozen appointments.

The pressure of an in-person presentation can seem daunting, but here are a few tips to help you on your way:

<u>Prepare a 3-Minute Presentation</u> –3 minutes may not sound like much time but, consider TV commercials. They get their message across in 30 seconds or less. 3 minutes for a 'gatekeeper', who does not know you, is enough time to decide whether they have interest. This means you are not going to play your game in these 3 minutes, but you can show them the basics of how your game plays.

Begin At The Beginning – set your game up first (which is not part of your 3 minute spiel). Package everything ahead of time in such a way that set up will go quickly and smoothly. While you are setting up, ask them, "Is there anything specifically you are looking for right now and are there any new directions you will be testing for next year?" This information can be very helpful in understanding the company and you may pick up a tip that can put you ahead of the curve for next year. Begin your demonstration with the name, tag line, number of players and age range. I have seen too many novices start their presentation in the middle of game play which leads to many questions from those watching. There is a logical sequence to the pitch and it is…

Spec Sheets – keep your spec sheet out and handy. Follow your pitch as if you are paraphrasing from your spec sheet: name, tag, etc. When you get to game play make sure you name the objective first. Then move on to describe how the game starts and walk the 'gatekeeper' through the phases of play to the game's final resolution.

Practice Makes Perfect – you can practice making a pitch by taking a published game you know how to play and teach the basic game play to someone else in under 3 minutes. Keep working at it until you can do it without sounding rushed and are able to flow from one segment to the next with ease. Then you can practice your pitch for your game.

Making Contact – it is important to make eye contact throughout your presentation. It is equally important to get the person you are presenting to involved in your game by putting them in contact with it. This could mean dealing them a few cards to hold, giving them playing pieces to move or stack, or having them perform certain aspects of game play. If you can get them participating in your demo, you increase your chances of them being interested in bringing in your game for evaluation.

Stack the deck – in your play tests, if you have noticed any of the sounds of success occurring under particular circumstances during the game, set your game up to repeat that success. You can purposely stack a deck so that the person you present to gets the funniest or best cards. If there is a particularly cool event that happens during the game, skip right to it so that everyone gets to experience it. Stage the presentation so the best elements of your game shine!

Hurry Up and Wait

What should you expect once you get the green light to send your prototype in for review? Be prepared to wait, and then wait some more.

You may pursue as many game companies as you like, as long as the number is equal to the quantity of prototypes you are willing and able to make. For example, if you can make three prototypes, you can approach three companies, and if one company passes, approach another in its place. You do not want to make a company that has committed to evaluating your game wait while you get a prototype back from someone else.

It is rare that you hear anything within the first month once a company has your prototype for review and it can be up to six months or more. The first few months of the year and the summer months are generally the busiest for game companies due to the number of trade shows that they attend at those times. Keep this in mind when doing follow-ups.

You may contact the companies to inquire about the status of the review as you wait, but it is best not to become a nuisance. If they ultimately pass, the majority of companies will return your prototype, but, sadly, there is no guarantee that you will get it back. You can provide postage for its return but still there is no guarantee. Always make sure your address is prominent and accessible on all your materials. Hopefully, they will include notes on their reason for passing. If so, keep these notes because they can help if you choose to redesign the game and re-pitch it at a later date.

Success

There is no excitement in game design that measures up to when the call comes through that a game company is interested in licensing your game.

What can you expect when striking a deal? As with all contracts, the various elements are up for negotiation — it is up to you to make the deal you can be comfortable with. The various deal points that I look for in a contract are outlined below, but for any larger questions or issues, please consult a legal professional.

DEAL POINTS

<u>Advance</u> – this is the up-front money given to you and is normally stated as an advance against future royalties. The range can be $500 to $10,000 (or possibly higher for the largest companies); generally it will be about $1000 for small and medium-sized companies and $5000 for larger companies. Factors that influence this amount are the size of the first print run of the game, and the anticipated wholesale price for the game.

The formula I like to use to gauge a 'fair' price is…

Advance = Qty 1ˢᵗ Run ÷ 2 x Wholesale Price x Royalty Percent

My formula is based on the game company selling half of the games they print in the first year and paying a royalty on that. Selling half of what they print is a conservative target for a company and so they generally will see the sense in your asking for this. As an example, let's say that a company is printing 5,000 games and you are getting 5% on a target wholesale price of $10 (a $20 retail price). Your percentage per game would be 50¢ multiplied by a half-run of 2,500 that would yield an advance of $1,250. Less expensive games and smaller print runs will justify a smaller advance while more expensive games and larger print runs can yield a higher advance.

<u>Royalty</u> – this is the percentage you will receive for each game sold, based on the wholesale price. 5% is standard but I have heard of the rare occasion when a designer received 10%. If your game is tied to a license, such as Star Wars, your range will be lower, generally from 1% to 3%, due to more who are sharing pieces of the pie. While this reduction in the royalty may seem significant, it usually works out okay for the game designer due to the greater visibility of the product producing a higher volume of sales.

There are two ways to a designer might be successful negotiating an extra percentage point. One is to take a smaller advance in exchange for a higher royalty and the other is to ask for a tiered percentage. A tiered percentage clause states that if sales exceed a certain number of units, your royalty increases. As an example, instead of 5%, you would receive 6% when sales exceed 25,000 games.

Payment term – royalties paid quarterly has been the industry norm, but there is an increasing number of companies who prefer to pay royalties twice yearly. Generally sales through the first 2 Quarters are the lowest of the year, increasing in Q3 and maximizing in Q4.

Contract Length – generally you will see terms of 3–5 years offered, which is often the length of time it takes to see whether your game is doing well. Make sure you are aware of and comfortable with the terms of the renewal and the causes for terminating the contract, should you need to.

Non-performance clause – make sure you have some guarantees in your contract. First, you need to make sure that a target release date guarantee is stated. If there are production problems or other significant delays that prevent your game from being made, you might have to wait until the contract expires to get it back. Second, if sales dwindle and the company loses interest in your game, it may be difficult to get your rights back. A performance clause states that if sales (dollars or units) fall below a certain number in one year, rights revert back to you. Make the target number very low (several hundred games, for instance), so the company you are negotiating with feels it is fair and easily obtainable.

Worldwide Rights – are you giving the company permission to sell only in the U.S., or limiting the territory to North America, or English-speaking countries, or…? Usually, granting a company broad geographic rights suggests they have international distribution in place or they are looking to sublicense your game to a publisher in another country. If they are going to sublicense, consider what the likelihood is that you will be able to make a deal on this game in other countries yourself. If the likelihood is high, you may want to hold out some territories from the contract, because your slice of the pie will be larger. For example, your publisher strikes a deal with a German company and is getting 7%. Of that 7%, you may get anywhere from 25% to 50%. If your chances of selling the game in another country are slim, then take the money and run. Getting more money for no additional work is usually a good thing. Typically, game companies have better connections and can have good success selling a game they have published and has some sales history.

Rights in All Media – does the contract say that you are assigning rights for a board game only, or does it mention other media, such as game shows, computer game, internet games, and cell phone games? As with worldwide rights, gauge your chances vs. the company's chances of selling the game into that medium. Again, more money for no extra work can be a good thing.

Name on the Box – Ask for your name to be printed somewhere on the game packaging, otherwise your parents may never believe that you invented it. My approach is to ask that my name be on the front, and then move to the back of the box if I meet resistance. In the worst case, I settle for my name in the rules. One way or another, make sure you are identified as the designer somewhere! You will be glad you did.

Copies of your game – for your first game especially, I would ask for a large quantity of free samples, like two dozen. You will want to give games to all the people that helped you along the way.

Request a clause that allows you to receive 3 more copies each year for as long as the game is in print. Down the line, if there are rule or art changes in a future print run, you will receive a current copy of the game. I usually also ask for a clause that allows me to buy quantities of the game at a better-than-wholesale price, which I might use for promotional giveaways or other marketing purposes.

Creative Review – ask to be a part of the design process, even if it is only to see the art before it goes to print. Ultimately the game company has final say, but you can offer valuable feedback on various design elements. It is especially important that you see the rules before they go to print because you know better than anyone else how your game plays, and a re-write could inintentionally lead to confusion, misinterpretation, and omissions.

WHEN CAN I RETIRE?

It is very difficult to accumulate a large quantity of money very quickly in game design or game publishing. Even if you come up with the next big hit, by the time the game is created to the time it ends up on the shelves of retail stores, it can be from 1–3 years. And then you have to wait until the game picks up speed and that could be an additional 3 years. It is not a quick process. And to make any significant money, the game has to break the 100,000 unit mark, and then there is no guarantee it will continue to sell at that pace. So having the chance to retire from game design is an opportunity afforded very few. It is possible to earn a living designing games, and even for the casual designer, earning a fairly steady extra income is not out of reach.

But if you are asking yourself the question, "When can I retire from game design?", I would say I have never heard other game designers talk about retiring. For us work is too much like play, so why stop? We create fun, we have fun, and we work with fun people. You would be hard-pressed to find a better job.

What's Next?

After your first game publishes, if you choose to continue, you will find it much easier to get your new game ideas in front of people and to schedule meetings. Instantly you become validated as a bona fide game designer.

If you are good enough to design one game that was licensed, then you can easily design another... and another. Imagine getting multiple checks every quarter instead of for just one game. The more games that reach market, the more chances you have that one of them will take off and bring in decent numbers.

Designing games is not about finding the needle in the haystack. Like playing a game, it is about increasing your chances of success. Becoming a game designer with more than one title under their belt is the choice that gives you the opportunity to get lucky in finding that 'needle'. Reading this book, I think, is an excellent start, and hopefully, the ideas contained in this book will further guide on your journey through this fantastic and joyful world.

It certainly has filled my days with fun and rewards, and I hope it can do the same for you. Happy journeys!

Appendix I

Some important websites for game inventors

www.gamedesigncentral.com – my website, filled with lots of useful inventor-related pages including a free monthly inventor newsletter, a list of handy sources, and game companies list. New items added frequently.

www.boardgamegeek.com – the largest gaming community website. A great game database and some good forums including one for board game design.

www.bgdf.com – stands for Board Game Designers Forum. As the name implies, a forum specifically for game inventors.

www.discovergames.com - provides very useful help for self-publishers wanting to do trade shows, and contains a broad array of info including an Inventor Help section.

two yearly educational forums aimed at toy and game inventors:
www.toyandgameinventors.com
www.tgifcon.com

Printed in the United States
By Bookmasters